Article Five:
Repairing American Government
Amid Debilitating
Partisan Strife

Scot Wrighton

Article Five:
Repairing American Government Amid Debilitating Partisan Strife

First Edition: 2023

ISBN: 9781524318499
ISBN eBook: 9781524328474

© of the text:
  Scot Wrighton

© Layout, design and production of this edition: 2023 EBL

Table of Contents

Introduction

The American people are at war with themselves. The political Right accuses the Left of immorality, deliberately tanking the economy, tagging them as "communists" and "unhinged" enemies of free speech. The Left brands the political Right as "racists," and "domestic terrorists," and ascribes apocalyptic consequences to their governance plans. Those who look past the name-calling and hyperbolic rants quickly discern a titan struggle for political power. Acquiring power at any cost is now the end game for the Left and the Right. In this escalating war of words, moderate, pragmatic, and reasoned voices are drowned out, overwhelmed by toxic vitriol from both sides.

This modern struggle is not about racism, "wokeism," exceptionalism, originalism, or any other "ism." It is fundamentally about political factions and their quest for power; this means the root cause is governance. The authors of the Constitution feared domestic, partisan factions more than they feared foreign invasion. If nations cannot contain factions and balance governance powers, then systems will collapse or become authoritarian. American government is now in danger of unravelling; but the good news is that America's governance system contains an undeployed cure for its self-inflicted partisan injuries. Hidden in plain sight, tucked neatly into the text of the

U.S. Constitution, is an antidote capable of bridling cancerous partisanship. The Constitution and constitutional law are the rules of engagement for the political blood sport perpetrated on a polarized country by the media, and many of the nation's top government officials. Recent Supreme Court decisions dealing with gun control, abortion, federalism and bureaucratic policymaking now serve to clarify, to the Right, Left, and Center, that the language of the Constitution really matters (of course, it has always mattered). That the Constitution, political power and governance are all at the center of today's partisan controversies may be hard to discern amid incendiary rhetoric spewed daily from CNN, MSNBC, and Fox News. Their polarizing rhetoric exacerbates divisive partisanship; but it continues because political, social and economic power are the prizes. This short little manual offers a roadmap for peace.

If the Constitution is broken, then it has to be fixed or the country goes on the rocks. To determine if the Constitution is really broken requires healthy debate about the specific activities, responsibilities, duties, and powers that should be, and should not be, within the ambit of State and Federal governments. The chasm separating advocates of all-inclusive "cradle-to-grave" Federal power, and those favoring "limited government," grows ever wider. The basic role of government in modern life, the practical logistics of 'separated' and 'limited' governmental powers, and how nationhood itself is sustained, are all in flux. The Constitution is the principal battleground; other skirmishes are just diversions. Thankfully, the Constitution includes an escape hatch—though it has never been used; it is a comparatively peaceful, consultative, and compromise-based alternative to disaster—an Article Five Convention.

Today's toxic political dialogues claim to be about election integrity, secure borders, energy policy, health policy, monetary policy, crime prevention, equity and identity politics; but all of these flashpoints are surrogates for the real issue: governance. The Left accuses the Right of not governing at all; but for the Left, governing means enacting sweeping and disruptive social and structural changes opposed by the Right—so the Left sees the Right's conservative (leave things alone) view of the world as no governance at all. The Right accuses the Left of legislating a new socialist order using tyranny, authoritarianism, and election manipulation. Amid this level of polarization, new substantive public policy rarely emerges from Washington. The Federal government has grown accustomed to, and tolerates, deadlock. Predictably, normal citizens grow angry and cynical with the endless stalemate, deepening hatreds, even among family members and workplace groups. Elections end in stalemate. The status quo no longer produces effective governance; it is non-governance, and it is not sustainable.

National governance rules are embodied in constitutions. Constitutions do not inherently favor large powerful governments, or weak ones. They do not, by design, advance individual rights and freedoms over government power. Constitutions provide the norms and architecture for governing politics—they are the rules of the game. Some constitutions include declarations of basic rights and freedoms governments cannot deny except in emergency circumstances; and some do not. Some constitutions create powerful unitary governments to which all sub-national local and provincial governments are entirely subservient, while other constitutions create complex systems of federalism by which states and other sub-national units operate, partially independent of central authorities, checking (or limiting) the power of the central government.

In 21st Century America, those favoring a ubiquitous role for government (when they are unable to achieve their political objectives) assert that their constituents are maligned, forgotten, and marginalized by the other side. Those favoring "limited government" (when they are unable to achieve their political objectives) assert that government is becoming tyrannical, intrusive, and authoritarian at the hands of the other side. Both factions believe democracy itself hangs in the balance unless their side prevails. Again, the underlying problem is not diversity, class struggle, or the role of traditional values; it is a dispute about governance—specifically the exercise of government power—and when and how it is used. When Federal Courts scolded the CDC, telling them they lack constitutional authority to require masks on airplanes, the media howled that the Court jeopardized public health and safety—when in fact, the rules of constitutional federalism simply do not invest the CDC with the power the media thinks they should have to govern.

Struggles over governance and political power are not new. The U.S. government has occasionally sought to self-limit its powers, and at other times grow their powers, since the late 18th Century. During two and one-third centuries, enlargements of government power were rationalized by wrapping them in new public policy virtues, or they were driven by war, financial necessity, popular demands, pragmatism and necessity, or the charismatic vision of a single leader. Regardless of the driver, without limits on the accumulation of power by a nation's central government, threats of tyranny, despotism, and abuse-of-power always loom. How then should the wielding of government power be altered so the ultimate authority to govern comes from The People? How can government's coercive influences be better balanced to prevent power abuses and preserve liberty?

The Constitution is the "how"; it is at the legal 'ground zero' of governance debates. Any national conversation about the proper roles for American government rapidly leads citizens to constitutional provisions. In America, We the People *can* reset the responsibilities of State and Federal governments, decide what activities and policies government should leave to others, and insert into foundational documents updated and modernized rules for joint governance, hopefully investing them with lasting legal impact and effect.

This book is a manual for the daunting task of adjusting and fixing American governance. An Article Five convention of states is not just another 'blue ribbon panel,' or town hall meeting, merely airing the views of its participants on topics of the day. It is an existing legal mechanism for compelling compromise. It has political force, it results in actual outcomes and consequences, and it has the legal 'teeth' to compel contesting political parties to meet together and find common ground.

To amend the Constitution, opposing parties must work with each other or risk failure. Every other alternative to an Article Five convention of states is a win-lose/lose-win outcome—either Democrats control the levers of power and get what they want; Republicans take the helm and get what they want; or more violence breaks out as factions believe peaceful means have failed. Democracy is NOT yet hanging in the balance. The fact our country remains together despite ugly partisan fighting is testament to the strength and resiliency of the Constitution. The Ship of State remains afloat. But quelling the fratricide may require revisions to the Constitution. Without them, violence and societal fraying will continue; and intense partisanship will lead to deeper fissures of the Union. Any process for peaceful repair of the Constitution requires compromise and cooperation. An Article Five convention of states will be contentious; but unlike partisan win-lose solutions, it is the only path capable of yielding peaceful outcomes, achieving consensus around a common set of political values, possessing a reasonable chance of implementation, and obtaining popular acceptance.

Chapter One makes an extended argument in favor of a convention of states and asserts there is no merit to warnings of modern Chicken Little pessimists who warn such a convention will produce a rogue and un-American document discarding traditional legal norms.

Chapter Two is a brief description of how Federal government power has grown since 1789. It illustrates how key original power-balancing structural provisions have been placed in the shadows over the years and marginalized, contributing directly to the modern fraying of constitutional checks and balances and partisan bickering.

Chapter Three is a practical guide for organizing and running a convention of states. This is a critical topic because Article Five of the Constitution provides no instructions on exactly how to manage a new constitutional convention. This lack of procedural guidelines leads some to think a convention of states is unmanageable. A convention of states will certainly need more than *Roberts Rules of Order* to succeed. In whatever way it is managed, an Article Five convention will need to be a robust forum for re-visiting the country's basic values. Some citizens, especially on the progressive Left, believe historic values should be overturned. So let the convention be a venue for fresh national governance discussions, and for discovering an updated governing consensus in an orderly way, using thoughtful constitutional amendment proposals.

Finally, Chapter Four offers twenty-five possible amendments a convention of states could initially consider, with specific wording for each proposed revision. Almost all of them have been discussed in some form in academic and popular publications since the 1950s, and more recently in electronic media.

An Article Five convention could be the last best hope for preserving the Union in these fractious times. It should be advanced in every state that has not called for one.

Chapter One

Why Do We Need a New Constitutional Convention?

More than ever before in the history of the American Republic, it is time to call a "convention of states" to update the U.S. Constitution, realize the nation's equal justice and due process creeds, re-align powers of the central government, re-assert the role of states in the country's Federal system, bolster freedoms and liberties contained in the Bill of Rights, ensure the U.S. Constitution remains a document modeling how to govern a diverse and pluralistic society, and update America's self-governing vision.

This lofty goal requires a constitutional convention because the Federal government has become leviathan and dysfunctional, acting contrary to the intentions of the authors of the Constitution, and this has produced the current partisan malaise. The authors of the Constitution sought to contain, de-fang, and dilute cancerous factions, because in a free and open society they cannot be eliminated. The Framers anticipated problems of faction and partisanship, but they could not have anticipated the way partisan factions have degraded the fabric of the Constitution and society itself in the 21st Century.

The U.S. Constitution is the oldest continually functioning constitution in the world, in part, because this 1780s era document fully acknowledges that power ultimately comes from The People—however much the Constitution blunts and mitigates this truth. It acknowledges that humans are flawed, that the human condition is fraught with foibles and selfishness, and that for these reasons the roles and powers of human governments should be limited in ways that compel flawed humans to work through their differences together, limit power accumulation by elites, compel broad compromises, encourage consensus, and thereby restrain natural avarice and evil.

The Constitution's authors understood that absolute power really does corrupt absolutely. Consequently, the 1787 Constitution combines the best features of a national government with those of confederations, to rein-in the power of potentially dictatorial chief executives. The Framers also understood that the shifting whims of a people's legislature should be tempered lest they succumb to short-lived popular trends. The document they produced disperses governmental power and prerogatives in ways intended to diffuse dictatorial and monarchical tendencies in favor of compromise and accommodation. The Constitution recognizes that some matters are better left to states; and it outlines how independent executive, legislative, and judicial branches can all 'check' each other, remain accountable to The People, and be accountable to each other, all at the same time.

Since the nation's founding, leaders entrusted with responsibility for executing the Constitution's precepts and provisions have not always acted faithfully, rendering the modern document imperfect. While virtuous, the Constitution is not flawless. It allowed slavery for nearly eighty years, and institutional racism for another century after the end of slavery. But it remains unsurpassed in its ability to manage competing interests, maintain access to due process for all, and frustrate dictatorial inclinations of would-be tyrants. It is still revered, not just in the United States, but around the world. However, the U.S. Constitution is not immutable or inerrant. It is a not God-breathed holy scripture standing universal for all time. The authors of the Constitution realized that despite their careful and considered authorship, revisions to the Constitution would be necessary in the future if this unique document was to successfully convey their bold new democratic experiment into the 19th Century, much less into the 21st Century and beyond. For this reason, the Constitution includes provisions for its own amendment.

The Constitution has been amended 27 times between 1791 and 1992. Excluding the Bill of Rights, these amendments have been comparatively narrow and surgical in scope. To date, the country has not seen fit to undertake a more comprehensive update of the Constitution. It has been tinkered with, but not overhauled, for 233 years. The process for approving narrow tinkering-type amendments, as well as for complete overhauls, is contained in Article Five. The language of Article Five's amendment process is short and succinct:

> **"The Congress, whenever two thirds of both Houses shall deem it necessary, shall propose Amendments to this Constitution, or, on the Application of the Legislatures of two thirds of the several States, shall call a Convention for proposing Amendments, which, in either Case, shall be valid to all Intents and Purposes, as Part of this Constitution, when ratified by the Legislatures of three fourths of the several States, or by Conventions in three fourths thereof, as the one or the other Mode of Ratification may be proposed by the Congress; Provided that no Amendment which may be made prior to the Year**

One thousand eight hundred and eight shall in any Manner affect the first and fourth Clauses in the Ninth Section of the first Article; and that no State, without its Consent, shall be deprived of its equal Suffrage in the Senate."

No "convention of states" has been called since 1789. The U.S. Constitution's 27 amendments were all approved by Congress and then endorsed by the requisite three-fourths of the states to lawfully become part of the Constitution. Despite its dormancy, an Article Five "convention of states" is not a relic lacking practical purpose in the 21st Century. The Founding Fathers knew exactly what they were doing when they included a "convention of states" in Article Five, and their intended use of a conclave for making amendments is just as relevant today as it was in the late 18th Century.

The need for a modern Article Five convention of states is warranted by growing imbalances and abuses of Federal power; but it is also necessary because the current state of political and governance dysfunction resembles the sort of degradation and deterioration of stable governance that an Article Five convention was first intended to correct—that is, if the annotations and convention notes of the Framers and their contemporaries are to be taken at face value. The intentions of the Founding Fathers live on in *The Federalist Papers*, in their private journals, and elsewhere.

The Federalist Papers are often cited as original legal commentary supporting and explaining the intent of the Constitution's provisions. *The Federalist Papers* are 85 separately published essays advocating ratification of the new Constitution. The essays were authored by two leading delegates to the 1787 Constitutional Convention (James Madison and

Alexander Hamilton) and John Jay (later the first Chief Justice of the Supreme Court). James Madison is often referred to as the father of the modern constitution because of his extensive notes from the convention and his advocacy of the 'Virginia Plan,' which was the initial framework of a new Constitution considered by the 1787 Convention. *The Federalist Papers* were distributed principally in New York during the state-by-state ratification process following the convention's submittal of the proposed Constitution to the states to counter vocal Anti-Federalist views arguing that the proposed constitution put too much power in the hands of a central government. Throughout *The Federalist Papers*, its authors mention specific provisions of the proposed constitution inserted to prevent tyranny and despotism (today these are called 'checks and balances'). Hamilton emphasized that the new country needed a central government capable of maintaining the Union, but in doing so, the proposed Constitution narrowly restricted the Federal government's reach to "enumerated powers," leaving all other powers to the States and to the people.

In addition to *The Federalist Papers*, minutes and notes kept by convention delegates help modern readers understand their original goals, intentions and motives. Chief among these is the extensive journal kept by James Madison. By examining these numerous documents, 21st Century citizens can determine where original principles depart from recent interpretations and practice, where governmental power, especially at the Federal level, has been accumulated in ways surpassing the intentions of the Founders, whether these variances warrant 21st Century amendments, and whether the creation of entirely new constitutional concepts should be advanced in a modern convention of states to restore balance and political cooperation.[1] Madison's notes have been used in this way ever since they were posthumously published in 1840.

Writing in Federalist #85, Alexander Hamilton (a proponent of strong central government) realized that "the persons delegated to the administration of the national government will always be disinclined to yield up any portion of the authority of which they were once possessed." In other words, Congress can be expected to oppose the national will when it comes to limiting powers of the Federal government; and for this reason, the wording of Article Five gives Congress no option whether to call a "convention of states" if the necessary three-fourths of the states properly call for such a conclave. National rulers "will have no option upon the subject," Hamilton wrote, "By the fifth article of the plan, the Congress will be obliged" to call the convention. Federalist #85 emphasizes that the wording of Article Five is "peremptory" and not discretionary. If any doubt remained, Hamilton writes "Nothing in this particular is left to the discretion of that body [Congress]. And of consequence all the declamation about the disinclination to a change vanishes in air." Before the Constitution was ratified, its authors predicted Congress would resist attempts to trim their powers, and for this reason the Constitution had to provide a way to circumvent Congress, whenever The People perceived the national government strayed too far from their governance lanes.

Opponents of the proposed Constitution published rebuttal editorials to *The Federalist Papers*, printed in a more piecemeal fashion in different publications between 1787 and 1790; only later, when compiled, did they become known as *The Anti-*

---

[1] There are many published accounts of the 1787 Constitutional Convention that rely on original notes. One of the most readable is: Larson, Edward, J. & Michael P. Winship, *The Constitutional Convention: A Narrative History from the Notes of James Madison*, New York: The Modern Library, 2005.

Federalist Papers. The authors of *The Anti-Federalist Papers* argued the proposed Constitution would lessen the power of states, lead to a tyrannical Federal government, and rule by elites unsympathetic to the lives of average citizens. The first set of *Anti-Federalist Papers* was published immediately following publication of the proposed Constitution, but the views of Anti-Federalists were already well known to constitutional convention delegates meeting in Philadelphia, and Article Five was likely written specifically to assuage fears of Anti-Federalists. If the national government became too powerful and overbearing, a convention of states could be convened to rein-in the abuse.

Thomas Jefferson was in France in 1787 and did not serve as a Constitutional Convention delegate; but early the same year, he wrote to James Madison asserting that "a little rebellion now and then is a good thing, and as necessary in the political world as storms in the physical."[2] The means and methods for a 'little rebellion' of the people to limit overreach by those in power would certainly include a "convention of states" in the minds of the Founding Fathers. All the Framers had a deep distrust of monarchial and centralized government. Their distrust was shared by an electorate that had just thrown off the tyranny of Great Britain in a protracted Revolutionary War. The numerous destructive national tyrannies that have ruled many of the world's nations during the 235 years since America's Constitutional Convention underscore the necessity of retaining legal mechanisms for checking and limiting national

---

[2]   Thomas Jefferson to James Madison, January 30, 1787, James Madison Papers, Founders Online, National Archives. "A little rebellion" was required, Jefferson wrote to Madison, to prevent "governments of force," and "a government of wolves over sheep."

governments as they expand, as they overreach, and eventually abuse their constitutional powers.

Jefferson did not advocate treason or the violent overthrow of the Federal government in his counsel to James Madison; but he realized the new nation's system of national governance should provide a mechanism for restraining elites in the ruling class from riding roughshod over the popular will—and do so without inciting factions to use armed rebellion for resolving their future conflicts. Article Five provides a legal and peaceful method to inject a 'little rebellion' into the Constitution's system of checks and balances—part of the brilliant system of checks and balances limiting abuse of power by ruling elites that has sustained American democracy ever since the nation's founding. Article Five was included precisely because its authors believed that while a central governance system for holding together the 13 former colonies was required, a new constitution still needed a mechanism to halt the Federal government's potential overreach, and to limit unwarranted expansions of national power made at the expense of The People and the States.

Proposals for a Second Constitutional Convention (convention of states) have been made throughout the nation's history for different reasons. In recent years, the use of a convention has been suggested to advance a balanced budget amendment, limit the influence of 'dark money' in elections, develop an alternative way of electing the president (possibly replacing the Electoral College), enact Congressional term limits, and adopt measures limiting the Federal government's ability to usurp State powers. Most of these proposals have enjoyed only minimal support among ruling classes and elites at the Federal level. Members of Congress have historically been disinclined to approve constitutional amendments limiting their power and prerogatives, just as Alexander Hamilton predicted in Federalist #85.

Sustained and concerted efforts were made in the 20th Century to call constitutional conventions in response to the Supreme Court's *Baker v. Carr (1962)* and *Reynolds v. Sims (1964)* decisions dealing with apportioning state legislative districts, and later to compel the addition of a balanced budget amendment to the Constitution. Both fell only a few states short. The serious possibility that enough states would call for a Second Constitutional Convention, however, has created pressure on Congress to give the people what citizens and states clamored for. In the early 20th Century, calls for direct popular election of senators was resisted by Congress until the movement for an Article Five convention of states was just one state short of the number required. Only then, in 1912, did Congress draft and submit to states what later became the 17th Amendment. Prior to the 17th Amendment, Senators were appointed by their state legislatures to serve in Congress' upper house. Only the threat of a convention of states forced Congress to approve an amendment providing for direct election of senators. But all of these 20th Century convention efforts were advanced in pursuit of narrow, single-topic surgical revisions to the Constitution. None sought broader overhaul. Forcing Congress' hand to make bigger structural changes is an unlikely outcome today because no consensus exists about how the Constitution should be modernized and updated. No 1912-type external threat can be mounted in support of fundamental structural changes because none have consensus support. There may be a widespread belief that comprehensive constitutional updates are needed, but it does not translate into a popular consensus for advancing any specific amendments.

While cynicism about the character of modern governance may be rife, there is no wide popular support for an entirely new Constitution either. Citizens are much more likely to support efforts to mend and repair the existing Constitution, as opposed to starting over. But the method for enacting minor amendments, as employed in the past, is not the best way to comprehensively update the entire document. Despite an abundance of proposals for new constitutional amendments in each session of Congress, no amendments advance to ratification because of the difficulty of obtaining a two-thirds majority for passage in both Houses of Congress. This hurdle could be avoided by calling a convention of states and bypassing Congress as the Founding Fathers intended; but this idea has been derided and ridiculed as a dangerous and unpredictable option. As a result, nothing happens, and governance dysfunction and rancorous partisanship worsens.

Article Five simply says Congress shall call a convention of states "for proposing amendments." It does not require amendments be of a common topic or policy category. Article Five provides no detailed guidance on how to interpret and enact the provision "the Application of the Legislatures of two thirds of the several States" to ascertain whether and exactly how state resolutions calling a Second Constitutional Convention should comply with Article Five (e.g., must all state resolutions be passed within the last five years or within the last fifty years?).

Extant notes from the 1787 convention suggest an Article Five convention of states was not primarily intended for crafting surgical revisions of a few sections, or dealing with narrow topics (like income taxes, direct election of senators, status of the District of Columbia, or presidential term limits). If more extensive corrections were thought necessary sometime in the future, the appropriate mechanism provided by the Constitution's authors was an Article Five convention. Excluding the Bill of Rights, the 11th thru to the 27th constitutional amendments have only limited scope and solve narrow problems. To date, the nation has not found it prudent to revisit the Constitution's "first governance principles" and has instead only advanced comparatively small and limited changes. A thorough and general revision of the entire Constitution can be peacefully accomplished only via a convention of states.

A modern convention of states will not operate in a vacuum sealed off from current events. The public will respond directly to a convention's progress, as reported by the media, and react to its deliberations. In this way, delegates will be able to gauge levels of popular support for amendment ideas. They will have the luxury of time to deliberate and reach decisions outside the bounds of Congressional rules and media deadlines in considering both broad and surgical revisions to the Constitution. They can take up structural and "first governance principle" reforms; and they can ponder whether their efforts collectively reflect a "sense of the people [in ways that] provide a system more consonant to it."[3] A minority of 1787 convention delegates sought to insert a requirement for a second convention of states into the Constitution, after some pre-determined number of years, precisely because they knew the Constitution would require changes to remain viable.[4] Such a re-evaluation is now long overdue.

A convention of states should not be feared. There are existing bulwarks to prevent crazy outcomes. The real danger is that special interests who benefit from leaving things as they are create barriers to necessary constitutional revisions capable of healing the country's current wounds. Then chaos ensues and tyranny is the result. Congress and the Executive Branch will resist an Article Five convention because it threatens their powers and prerogatives.

---

[3] George Mason, in Larson and Winship, op. cit., p. 152-53.

[4] Jefferson wrote again to Madison on September 6, 1789: "the Earth belongs to the living, not to the dead, so the Constitution should be refreshed every generation." See the Madison Papers. An every-century convention of states is recommended in Chapter Four, below.

If two-thirds of the states have met the process requirements to call a convention, however, Congress has no discretion in the matter. Congress will likely resist anyway by objecting to the different times, and the different circumstances, under which states approved resolutions calling for a convention of states; or they may object on the grounds that different states passed resolutions dealing with different topics. Article Five does not require identical state resolutions or the same amendment topics.

If Congress resists or ignores a 34-state call for a convention, then the resulting impasse may require resolution by the Supreme Court. The Court can resolve issues as diverse as the timing of state resolutions, whether states can rescind an earlier convention call, determine delegate eligibility and more; but courts probably cannot legally compel Congress to call a convention as directed by Article Five. It is not for Congress to decide if the time has come to revise the Constitution—this decision rests with the States. Congress must only act ministerially to call the convention "for proposing Amendments." When the time comes, Congress will likely be torn between its inherent tendency to protect its powers, on the one hand, and its constitutional obligation to convene a convention of states, on the other. If Congress accepts its constitutional responsibility, it could determine the venue of the Second Convention, how each state is represented, establish deadlines for preparation and submittal of amendments, and at least attempt to provide some recommended parameters for the conclave's agenda.

Common Cause and other organizations are on record opposing a convention of states—largely because they believe such a convention may not be constrained to enumerated topics and because the brief language of Article Five contains no procedural rules for the management of the convention. They worry that a "runaway convention" could produce an entirely new document or amendments to the existing Constitution that are very different from what the legislatures calling for a "convention of states" intended—just as the original 1787 Constitutional Convention arguably went beyond its mandate to repair the Articles of Confederation.

Opponents of a "convention of states" are largely correct that the convention would have very few fixed and pre-established agenda parameters—other than the constitutional constraint that they are called only to *amend* the existing document. But this is not sufficient reason to discard the checks-and-balances mechanism of a convention of states. The fearmongering about an Article Five convention of states is without merit.

The original 1787 Constitutional Convention adopted their own rules, and subsequently produced a masterful document of national governance still revered throughout the world. A large percentage of Americans believe their Constitution is just fine the way it is, or that it requires only limited modifications. Very few Americans support throwing it out. The Revolutionary War-era Articles of Confederation did not enjoy this level of support, and they certainly had not achieved worldwide admiration.

There are several existing mechanisms (formal and informal) for ensuring a "convention of states" cannot become rogue and enact new constitutional measures hostile to American tradition and jurisprudence.

First, while the 1787 Constitutional Convention was called by the Continental Congress to broadly develop an alternative to the unpopular, weak and cumbersome Articles of Confederation, a 21st Century "convention of states" will likely have narrower goals and objectives. In 1787, convention delegates were creating a new country; a 21st Century convention of states would have no such mandate. Delegates to a modern convention would be selected to reflect each state's views about how the existing

Constitution should be updated and amended, **not** how to form a new nation. Almost all states will give specific instructions about the topics their appointees (or elected delegates) would be authorized to advance. Modern states' joint resolutions calling a Second Constitutional Convention list specific amendment provisions each state desires. Some of these resolutions already include detailed delegate instructions. State instructions may not be legally binding; but in the aggregate they would still constrain the convention's agenda. Detailed lists of amendments for consideration from states have no parallel in the 1787 convention. Today, states might even recall or replace their delegates in the event they strayed too far from state instructions. If delegates are elected rather than appointed, then the rhetoric of their campaigns will politically contain their actions at the convention. Finally, it is highly unlikely, and effectively impossible, that ANY state (much less three-fourths of them) would send delegates to a 21st Century Constitutional Convention with instructions to completely discard the existing Constitution.

Second, the language of Article Five specifically says a "convention of states" can only consider *amendments*.

Third, delegates will know there is too much at stake for any other outcome than consideration of multiple amendments. Delegates gathering in Philadelphia in 1787 all understood the shortcomings of the Articles of Confederation—though they had vastly different ideas about how to fix them. Now, after 233 years of use, and despite its antiquated features, there remains great respect for the U.S. Constitution among persons of all political persuasions, such that it would be extremely difficult to throw out the entire Constitution, particularly when several carefully crafted amendments would be less disruptive and more palatable.

Fourth, in the highly unlikely event of a rogue convention, or one succumbing to radical factions and espousing tenets far from the mainstream of American political thought, it is certain their work product would fail to secure the required approval of three-quarters of the states—in which case, the existing Constitution would remain in full force and effect, unchanged. Approval from three-fourths of the states is a very high bar for approval—it is meant to force competing factions to find compromise and only adopt provisions enjoying wide bipartisan support. In fact, securing ratification from 38 states will require more than just compromise; it will likely require near-consensus from the delegates, with supporting ideas and principles that are easily communicated to the general public, on both the political Left and Right.

Fifth and finally, a 21st Century convention of states could not rely on practical necessity to obtain ratification of radical and unpopular amendments. Rhode Island sent no delegates to the Constitutional Convention of 1787, and they were the 13th and last state to ratify the constitution in 1790—long after the other twelve states. In the end, Rhode Island ratified the Constitution not because they liked it, but because they had nowhere else to go. No state would feel a similar imperative today. If recommendations of a modern convention of states failed to obtain a three-fourths majority, then the country will continue to operate under the current system. There would be no threat to a state's existence due to failure to ratify, as Rhode Island faced in 1790. New amendments will succeed or fail in state ratification votes entirely on their merits, and not because a slim majority of states can back a minority of states into a corner.

Six times in U.S. history well-meaning and high-minded proposals to amend the Constitution have emerged from Congress with the requisite two-thirds majority support, only to fall short when submitted to the States. It is extremely difficult to attain approval by three-fourths of the States to do anything—much less amend the Constitution. Delegates to a 21st Century "convention of states" will likely remind each other repeatedly of the difficulty of achieving this level of agreement (as did the 1787 convention delegates). By itself this requirement will weed-out crazy proposals, thwart radical factions in the convention, and compel delegates to find popular compromises.

Without compromise a modern convention of states will be doomed to failure. This is the beauty, and the genius, of deploying an Article Five convention of states at this point in the nation's history. Compromise is in short supply in our nation's capital today—but a convention of states cannot function without compromise. Delegates will have no choice but to seek and forge workable compromises, and eventually mature these compromises into a new public consensus for 21st Century governance.

Finding compromise will be difficult—especially because the political Left and Right are so divided. A Second Constitutional Convention may have to spend several months just talking and debating with each other before they can draft a single amendment (just as delegates did in 1787). Keeping such a fractious convention focused on creating a better constitution, one capable of lasting for another century or two, will be a difficult procedural, management and political challenge. Delegates will each bring their deeply held views to the convention. For this reason, this book dedicates all of Chapter Three to discussing convention management and procedural matters.

After the 1787 Constitutional Convention completed its work, it took another year and a half to obtain ratification from three-fourths of the states, and to conduct the first Federal election selecting George Washington as the first president and electing the nation's first Congress. President Washington was inaugurated in April 1789, and the rest is history. The post-1789 history of America saw a relentless increase in the power, scope, and reach of the central government. Understanding the forces that drove this enlargement of central government power, up to the present, is the topic of Chapter Two. This is relevant to the consideration of new constitutional revisions, because if the march of American history created constitutional misalignment, then understanding the source of the dysfunction informs modern strategies for repairing stress-cracks and imbalances.

Balance of power (so called "checks and balances") was a key aim of the Constitution because the document had to act as a barrier to tyranny. Delegates to the 1787 Constitutional Convention likely would have asserted that if the final document they labored to produce frustrated tyrants, dictators, and disruptive factions seeking to use the power of government to advance policies affronting freedom and liberty, then the Constitution was functioning as it should. But if the Constitution thwarted compromise, bipartisanship, effective governance, and the balance of power, then a convention of states should be convened to repair the nation's system of governance.

Benjamin Franklin's confidence in the finished Constitution was guarded. He predicted America would "be well administered for a course of years, and can only end in despotism . . . when the people shall become so corrupted as to need despotic government."[5] In short, if the Constitution did not work, The People would welcome tyranny if they thought it would end chaos and corruption. Franklin was right; without effective and constitutionally balanced governance, tyranny naturally fills the resulting void. Good governance requires occasional maintenance and revision. The authors of the Constitution understood America's initial fragility, and they knew that to avoid abuse of power, Federal overreach, dangerous factions (i.e.,

---

[5]   Benjamin Franklin, in Larson and Winship, op. cit., p. 154.

intense partisanship) and descent into civil disorder, the new governance system would need to be amended periodically.

The U.S. Constitution is an international model for good governance precisely because national constitutions elsewhere have rarely achieved this goal of balancing, diffusing and decentralizing power while still maintaining national unity. By contrast, in Turkey and Russia in the 21st Century, national leaders used constitutional amendments to centralize power and bolster dictatorial control. In both cases, Turkish and Russian dictators argued their tyrannical actions advanced the greater public good. In places like Myanmar and North Korea, there have never been true constitutional documents in place to constrain dictators and oligarchies. Lacking such guardrails, these countries are among the worst examples of abuse of power and poor governance by elites; both border on being "failed states." Justifying tyranny in the interests of short-term goals never ends well. Popular "ends" do not justify tyrannical "means" in national governance. In Israel and modern Germany, by contrast, there has never been a serious attempt to re-write constitutional checks and balances to better facilitate the growth of tyranny. There remains sufficient historical memory to restrain those who would give the German Chancellor too much power.

In the United States, those who believe Democrats failed to undermine and overturn the 2016 General Election results, and those who believe Republicans failed to undermine and overturn the 2020 General Election results, both point to the Constitution's resiliency, its power-disbursing checks and balances, and its structure of state-to-nation federalism, to support their respective claims. They are both correct. The very definition of American 'federalism' derives from the Constitution's merger of confederated and national governments.[6] The fact that both

---

[6] Federalist #39 explains that the Constitution does not create a national government, but rather a uniquely (for 1787) American federal system.

the political Right and Left use the Constitution's provisions to 'check' their political opponents re-enforces the Constitution's efficacy and the practical merit of its 'balance of power' principles. But the existing constitutional fabric has nonetheless frayed.

Proposals to nationalize elections, federalize local police, pack the Supreme Court solely for the purpose of working around Congress to obtain partisan political victories, use the Federal government's power-of-the-purse to neuter local zoning and land use controls, meddle in local school district policies, elevate presidential orders into binding legal edicts and fiats, and deploy a new definition of 'equity' to further neuter the meaning and intent of the 9th and 10th Amendments ("reserving" all powers not specifically given to the Federal government "to the States respectively, or to the People"), collectively comprise dysfunctional abuse-of-power circumstances resembling what Founding Fathers and authors of the Constitution feared. The Founding Fathers were not clairvoyant, but they suspected that if structural revisions to the Constitution became necessary due to new power imbalances, then enacting changes would require the initiative of persons outside government using a process capable of functioning independent of the central government, without support from entrenched ruling elites.

Not all the states currently calling for a 'convention of states' want a Second Constitutional Convention for the same reasons. But today, there is a broad belief that the Federal-State government relationship, including the power and reach of both levels, needs revision for the country to meet the challenges of the 21st Century. In short, both the Left and the Right acknowledge there are structural governance problems that cannot be resolved just by one or two narrowly worded constitutional amendments. The Left and the Right probably agree on little else.

Effective governance in a pluralistic republic requires "The People", from whom power is ultimately derived, be sufficiently educated, and civically informed about how to formulate and adopt public policy. But in modern America, an astonishingly large percentage of the population do not even know what the three branches of government are, much less how they check and control one another. A second convention of states would create a national dialogue about governance and the Constitution such that, regardless of whether public schools restored civics to their high school curricula (and despite what amendments are produced), American citizens would be better educated about governance and citizens' role in running American government.

America's Federal government is incapable of restricting its own powers. Congress has no interest in adopting term-limits, or strengthening the 10th Amendment, or adopting a constitutional amendment to balance the budget, because all these proposals reduce the power of the central government. Americans, however, do not respect leaders who relentlessly pursue more power for themselves. This is one of the reasons respect and confidence in the Federal government is at an all-time low (regardless of the political party in control of the White House or Congress). Despite constant enlargement of Federal power, over generations, Congress and Washington DC, still cannot heal themselves—so partisanship and polarization spread, becoming more cancerous. Amid the stalemates, government elites devise extra-constitutional 'work-arounds' thereby creating more governance power imbalances. The nation's political dialogue today is toxic, divisive, and ultimately destructive of democratic/republican governance itself.

In a country where political power is nearly equally divided, where the Left and the Right increasingly make wilder claims about the destructive motives of the other (yelling more loudly at, and past, each other), there seems little hope for peaceful resolution. American society continues to sink into permanent polarization, where every topic is viewed through a partisan lens.

With providential wisdom, delegates to the 1787 Constitutional Convention devised a mechanism allowing The People to amend the Constitution without the approval of Congress. This mechanism is the remedy for extreme partisanship and political polarization—because a Second Constitutional Convention will force the Left and the Right to come together and compromise, negotiate, reconcile and find common ground, without which neither side can expect any degree of long-term success. A convention of states is the constitutional equivalent of parents telling squabbling siblings to go into the same room, shut the door, and not to come out until they have settled their differences and figured out how to get along with each other.

This is the cathartic remedy for mending current divisions that have pitted citizen against citizen for years. This is no longer about the death of civility; that 'ship has sailed.' The Right and the Left must do more than learn to be nice to each another. Politeness and civility can get combatants through staged social gatherings, but they cannot address the underlying problem—the Right and Left have fundamentally different world views and governance expectations. As a result, these two titan factions must find common points of reference. Only then can the country begin to mend the fabric of government and society itself.

The United States needs a solution that goes to root causes and core issues. The country's quality of governance has deteriorated because the architecture of governance has been manipulated to advance divergent political values and world views, rather than provide safety, security, rule-of-law and continuity. There is no durable governance solution to be found in one side prevailing over the other. Bringing warring factions together and compelling them to enact changes with near consensus levels of support through an Article Five convention will not award the status of "winner" to one side and the label of "loser" to the other. To be successful, an Article Five convention must produce an updated method of governance in which a super-majority of Americans can have a renewed sense of faith and confidence in the future, and where the country can together envision a sustainable system of self-governance.

Chapter Two

How the Federal Government Grew to Be So Powerful & Out-of-Balance

The Federal government's reach and scope are greater now than at any time in history. The ubiquitous power of the modern Federal government extends far beyond parameters first set by the Constitution. Some government expansion has been good for the country, and some has not. The Founding Fathers sought to avoid an impotent and ineffective central government, like the one they had under the Articles of Confederation; but they also feared excessive Federal power. Consequently, central government power was originally limited to providing for the common defense, maintaining the rule of law, regularizing commerce between states, and protecting fundamental rights in a union of states. This chapter is a brief overview of changes in government scope and power since 1789. It illustrates how the Constitution's original balance-of-power arrangement has become imbalanced in the 21st Century and highlights key provisions of the Constitution that have been subjected to reinterpretation, reinvention, and neglect in ways that have brought the country to the unrestrained and deeply divisive partisanship it faces today.

The United States was an agrarian country in 1789, espousing a new mantra of equal opportunity for all who were willing to work hard—although this opportunity extended only to Caucasian, property holding men at the time. To become an international superpower, build the largest economy in the world, expand the franchise to nearly all adult citizens, and truly realize its goal of equal opportunity in a pluralistic and multi-cultural society over the following 230+ years required occasionally re-imagining constitutional federalism. It required that the Constitution stretch to meet the changing needs of a growing nation, provide justice to disenfranchised residents, and do all of this without becoming unmoored from its original conceptual framework of limited government in a union of multiple states, all of whom possess their own powers.

Massive enlargement of Federal power over time is not entirely responsible for the nation's current malaise. There are other causes. The Constitution has regularly failed to deliver on its promises of equal opportunity and equal voice—a factor contributing to consistent polling through Red and Blue Administrations—indicating that large majorities of Americans believe the country is on the wrong track. But if too much power has been shifted to a faraway capitol, and it causes most citizens to feel impotent and ignored, this also contributes to "wrong track" polling results. National histories from other countries amply illustrate that drifting toward an all-powerful unitary national government eventually tramples freedom and individual liberties. The loss of reasonable state and local discretion makes people feel powerless, and it causes citizens to stop trusting their national government, thus producing "wrong track" polling results.

In America, the drift toward constitutional imbalance occurred very gradually. The Revolutionary War was fought to throw off a tyrannical English monarch who ignored freedoms and liberties to which colonists believed they were entitled. The Declaration of Independence, and the Revolution itself, were both about protecting liberty. But when war ended, practical problems of competing special interests, soothing and holding together regional factions, managing foreign affairs, and determining the correct role of government in maintaining basic order were more on the minds of delegates to the Constitutional Convention of 1787. Then, delegates focused less on individual freedoms and liberty, and more on the architecture and functional mechanics of governance. They needed something to replace the Articles of Confederation. Under the Articles of Confederation, Congress had no power to levy taxes and no power to regulate foreign or interstate commerce; there was no national court system and no executive branch to implement the laws of Congress. Federalists prevailed in creating a new structure of governance, and the Constitution bears the imprint of Federalists like Washington, Adams, Hamilton, and others who argued for a strong central government, bolstered by liberal and flexible interpretations of the Constitution's enumerated powers, and assigning basic functions and powers to State and Federal governments. But the new Constitution also incorporated the views of moderate Anti-Federalists who later formed the "Democratic-Republican Party" (Jefferson, Madison, Monroe and others) asserting stricter and narrower interpretations of the Constitution's enumerated powers. These two groups sought to find a middle path between monarchy and pure democracy—because neither monarchy nor pure democracy was trusted by either camp of Founding Fathers.

Delegates to the first constitutional convention included prominent "Federalists" who believed a strong central government was necessary to hold the new nation together. But because the Constitution they produced included no protections for basic human rights, the "Anti-Federalists," who were suspicious of a strong central government, asserted that the proposed

Constitution was a conspiracy against the supremacy of the states and the free exercise of individual liberties. Anti-Federalists argued the new Constitution lacked a Bill of Rights delineating those individual and fundamental rights that would be "off-limits" to governments operating under a new Constitution.[7]

For its own political survival in 1789, the new Federal government fulfilled its ratification promises made during state-by-state approval of the Constitution and voted to limit themselves by adding a Bill of Rights to the new Constitution. By early 1789, the new Constitution had been approved by enough states to secure ratification, but not enough to ensure sustained legitimacy. Some states had ratified the new Constitution because delegates promised that in the First Session of Congress a Bill of Rights would be proposed for addition to the Constitution and sent to states for ratification. Two states (Rhode Island and North Carolina) refused ratification until the Bill of Rights was submitted. The Massachusetts ratification vote was contingent upon adoption of a Bill of Rights. Had the First Congress failed to write and submit a Bill of Rights to the states for ratification, it likely would have led to the calling of a Second Constitutional Convention just two years after the first (as provided by Article Five) to achieve this end. The Bill of Rights was ratified in December 1791, thereby codifying a declaration of basic rights and adding legitimacy to the entire Constitution (although key Federalists thought such a document unnecessary, as many state constitutions already included these rights).

Action to limit the powers of the Federal government in constitutional law with a Bill of Rights was one of the few acts

---

[7]   Lepore, Jill, *These Truths: A History of the United States*, W.W. Norton & Company, 2018, p. 129.
    See also DeRose, Chris, *Founding Rivals, Regnery History*, 2013, pp. 251-63

of restraint in an otherwise steady march toward enlarging the powers and reach of the Federal government. But adoption of the Bill of Rights was less an act of self-restraint than a decision driven by political compromise—the first of many that slowly changed the character of the national government. Despite the addition of the Bill of Rights, Anti-Federalists continued to believe that if the central government grew to be too powerful, individual rights and liberties would eventually suffer. For more than two centuries, balancing rights, liberties, individual freedoms, and demands for state autonomy with the practical demands of governance has been the backdrop for countless policy debates.

In 1791, Congress and President Washington approved legislation creating the first national bank. The Constitution does not provide for the creation of a national bank. But Treasury Secretary Alexander Hamilton believed this action to be lawful because it facilitated national commerce and was (he argued) permitted by Article 1, Section 8 of the Constitution wherein Congress is permitted to enact new laws found to be "necessary and proper" for carrying out the other powers. However, Thomas Jefferson and James Madison opposed the bill because the creation of a national bank was not specifically listed among Congress' enumerated powers in Article One. The bank was created anyway, but its charter was allowed to lapse in the early 1800s. A second national bank charter, approved by Congress in 1816, was also allowed to lapse after 20 years, in part because Federal power to create the bank was not specifically enumerated in the Constitution. Debates about banking, transport, education, social welfare, and countless other topics over the years, all possessed this common feature: should the Federal government's power to insert itself into new policy areas be limited to specifically enumerated powers in the Constitution, or was an expansion of Federal power implied?

National banking, upheld by the Supreme Court's 1819 *McCulloch v. Maryland* case, did not resolve collective and constitutional ambivalence about the Federal government's control over banking. But the *McCulloch* case established that Federal law is superior to state law. At its heart, the national bank dispute was about state sovereignty and determining how much Federal interference in state banking should be permitted. This debate played out for much of the 19th Century as American federalism evolved. Not until the 1913 creation of the Federal Reserve was the matter resolved through creation of an autonomous Federal Reserve, with a board of governors appointed by the president for fixed terms to partially insulate the Federal Reserve from politics. This was the tenuous compromise, after more than a century of argument, giving the Federal government new extra-constitutional powers to manage the economy. America largely accepted the compromise in order to reduce economic panics, recessions, and financial crises that had hobbled economic progress in the 19th Century; but it still increased the power of the central government. There are still people who believe the Federal Reserve wields too much power and does so beyond the authority of the Constitution.

Creating America's version of federalism was never about achieving optimum and efficient governance, or the best ways to deliver essential services. It was a series of political compromises to help hold the Union together and grow the nation, all while maintaining a delicate power balance between states and the national government. Should the Constitution be liberally construed to say that since Congress has the power to regulate interstate commerce and provide for the general welfare, that the country needs national banking mechanisms to achieve these ends? If not, is the government rendered impotent; if so, what are the limits of 'liberal construction' in interpreting constitutional provisions—limits intended to avoid sliding toward financial tyranny and usurpation of states' rights? If political or economic necessity is sufficient reason for wrecking constitutional balances, then it renders the 'limited government' provisions and principles of the Constitution hollow and meaningless. Of course, it is also reasonable to assert that what 'balance of power' looks like in the 21st Century should be different than what it looked like in the 18th Century. Whatever the governance parameters, without some kind of 'balance-of-power' structures, the Constitution cannot function properly.

Delegates to the First Constitutional Convention likely did not use the term, but what they struggled with throughout the summer of 1787 were basic questions of assigning specific "plenary" and original powers, wielded separately and jointly by both state governments and the national government. National supremacy and state autonomy had to be workably balanced in the new Constitution for it to be ratified. Delegates knew, but could not control, the extent to which time, politics, necessity, and legal or cultural evolution would alter initial interpretations of constitutional provisions through "liberal construction" of plenary powers. "Liberal construction" is the principle that the power to legislate on any matter should be interpreted broadly to include the power to legislate on all ancillary matters (i.e., items that are "necessary and proper" to the main object).

In 1803, the Supreme Court in *Marbury v. Madison* declared parts of the Judiciary Act of 1789 unconstitutional. This was the first time the high court pronounced that Congress could not pass laws changing, or conflicting with, the Constitution, and it firmly established that the Supreme Court was the final voice on whether laws are constitutional. This power is not expressly stated in the Constitution, but the court asserted it is implied, and can be liberally construed from the text. The *Marbury* case has served as a powerful check on the use of Federal executive and legislative power ever since; but it did not stop the growth of the Federal government.

When the United States was still a young nation, Americans generally wanted a unified and vibrant country—not separate sovereign states warring with each other—especially after concluding a second war against Great Britain (the War of 1812) where the need for common defense and strength in numbers was underscored. The country was still very vulnerable in the early 1800s; the British burned parts of Washington in 1814. It was also growing rapidly—with parts of the frontier chronically difficult to govern. Within 30 years of Constitutional ratification and the addition of the Bill of Rights, the United States doubled its territorial size, added two new amendments to the Constitution correcting defects discovered in the original version, and began to confront the reality that sectional differences were brewing capable of tearing apart the large and sparsely populated country, rendering it impossible to govern.

The presidency of Andrew Jackson, starting in 1829, increased the role of the Federal government largely because of the character of the White House occupant. The nation's seventh president advocated for enlarged suffrage, manifest destiny in the West, and aggressive policies to expand the nation into the western frontier, as well as policies spurning traditional eastern moneyed interests. Jacksonian Democracy relied on a powerful chief executive and popular support from non-elites. President Jackson was the nation's first populist leader; he vetoed more legislation than the first six presidents combined and contributed to the growing power of the Executive Branch—especially in the territories. Jackson owned slaves, ridiculed abolitionists, and dealt cruelly with Native Americans. He was among the most autocratic and dictatorial of 19th Century presidents.[8] But Congress and the electorate largely tolerated his assumption of greater power because Jackson was popular, solved thorny problems others could not, and he argued that his leadership style fit the needs of a growing country with a large and unmanaged frontier. Jackson's presidency was not democracy's finest hour, and it illustrated that the citizenry will sometimes opt for limited doses of authoritarianism instead of endure chaos and ineffective governance.

Laissez-faire government looked too much like governance by neglect, so Jackson offered a strong hand at the helm. During Jackson's presidency, the power of the Executive Branch grew simply because he took power where he needed to do so in an effort to advance his agenda. Several presidents after Jackson increased the power of the Executive Branch in similar fashion just by asserting authority over activities on which the Constitution was largely silent, even though the Constitution itself specifically deferred unmentioned powers to the states and to The People via the 9th and 10th Amendments. Sadly, Jackson did not use his considerable leadership skills to make any course corrections averting the coming constitutional crisis surrounding slavery.

Senator Henry Clay's American Whig Party sought to change presidential power in ways that stretched the fabric of the Constitution in different ways. American Whigs emerged in the 1830s offering what Clay called "the American System," a form of mercantilism[9] favoring tariffs to protect domestic industry, a

---

[8]   See H.W. Brands, *Andrew Jackson: His Life and Times*, Doubleday, 2005.

[9]   Mercantilism is an economic theory that trade generates wealth and that government should encourage trade because it serves the national interest through protectionism. In short, governments use their economies to augment state power at the expense of other countries. The primary

national banking system to foster more commerce, and increased spending on infrastructure to aid in the expansion of trade. Whigs believed this philosophy would bind the nation together and dissolve brewing sectional disputes. In the interests of diluting regional rivalries, Whigs were willing to overlook whether the Constitution explicitly authorized their "American System." The authority to levy protectionist tariffs is clearly a Federal power in the Constitution, but debate continued over the constitutionality of national banking and funding of large multi-state infrastructure projects. These were not yet settled law. Whig presidents (William Harrison, John Tyler, Zachery Taylor and Millard Fillmore) advanced mercantilism with limited success; but like Jackson, they were often overwhelmed by the growing sectional disputes eventually leading to Civil War. Senator Clay's much-heralded compromises managing the admission of new states were just proxy debates over slavery, and only served to delay the onset of the Civil War. From 1840 to 1860, the drift to war overshadowed constitutional arguments about how much power the Federal government should possess to advance trade, commerce, large infrastructure projects, and settlement of the Frontier.

The same debate resumed after the Civil War, as President Andrew Johnson rejected mercantilism, arguing that high tariffs might help big business, but they increased the costs of normal goods for the working class. Johnson also opposed the Federal government's involvement in building national roads and canals as unconstitutional because they were not specifically enumerated in the Constitution. He believed they were properly within the purview of the states, and he believed that if government intervened too much, it would destroy America's self-reliant spirit. His restraint was interpreted by his opponents

---

indicator of mercantilism's success is a favorable balance of trade (exports over imports).

as sympathy for the defeated South. For this reason, most of his vetoes suffered overrides, and his views were not shared by his successors. Much later in the 20th Century, President Hoover, and others, similarly decried increases in Federal power. The pattern was not hard to detect: the political factions in power liberally construed constitutional provisions to advance greater Federal power to achieve their political objectives; the parties out of power bemoaned the loss of self-reliance, reduction of state discretion, and limitations on individual freedom resulting from new policies that stretched the Constitution and added new national powers.

The Federal government's power to build and finance large multi-state infrastructure projects, like the National Road, was challenged as lying beyond the pale of the Constitution. The constitutional debate was not about roads, but about what authority was specifically granted to the Federal government in the Constitution to construct interstate roads and canals. The language of the Constitution allows the Federal government to "regulate commerce" and to "establish post roads" facilitating mail service. But does this provide authorization for interstate roads, railways and canals? In the end, the pre-Civil War Congressional governance compromise concerning large multi-state infrastructure projects evolved into an extra-constitutional system whereby states had to consent to Federal improvements made inside their jurisdictions—a system that, in part, remains in place to the present. Again, an increase in Federal power was borne out of necessity and practicality to facilitate the growth of the country.

The American Civil War, and its aftermath, entirely changed the trajectory of the Constitution and American federalism. Wars always increase the powers of central governments because the survival of the nation is at stake. Emergency powers are required to mobilize troops, produce munitions, resist insurrection, and maintain supply lines. But the fabric of the U.S. Constitution was altered by more than wartime exigencies in the middle of the 19th Century—because the constitutional contradictions of slavery had never been resolved during the previous 70 years. Civil war was the nation's reckoning for this procrastination. By 1860, constitutional contradictions could no longer be ignored.

Many Founding Fathers acknowledged slavery was irreconcilable with principles contained in the Declaration of Independence and the Constitution. Some of these men knew an inflection point would come in the 19th Century when the economic interests of the South crashed head-long into doctrines of human rights.[10] In 1787, however, they believed the problem could be resolved peacefully and gradually—they were tragically wrong. The origins of civil war, arguably, date from 1787 when the Framers were willing to engage in legal and moral gymnastics—in the interests of creating a new country.

Had slave states, in the 1840s and 1850s, been content to protect slavery only within the future Confederate states, the scourge of slavery may well have died out more gradually in the South—perhaps not until late in the 19th Century as it did in other parts of the world. But rather than defend slavery only where it was entrenched, by attempting to move more power back to states, the leaders of the future Confederate States of America tried to enlarge the power of the Federal government for purposes of protecting, reinforcing, and justifying slavery throughout the entire country, including its sparsely populated

---

[10] Several published works record this reticence, including those by Benjamin Franklin, Alexander Hamilton, John Jay and John Adams. Jefferson acknowledged closer to his death in 1826 that civil war was coming over the issue of slavery.

territories. Slavery was bad enough, but the South would not be content until the rest of the country was compelled to embrace and morally approve of race-based involuntary lifetime servitude. In 1860, candidate Abraham Lincoln chastised the South for their willingness to upend the Constitution in the interests of political expediency, to protect slavery, and even demand that the entire population pronounce slavery 'good.'[11] It was all a bridge too far and it ignited civil war.

During the Civil War, President Lincoln took unprecedented actions to expand the powers of the central government in the interests of preserving the Union and winning the war. As the war drew to a close and the nation transitioned to "Reconstruction," constitutional inconsistencies that had allowed slavery to exist (like counting slaves as three-fifths of a person), were finally corrected by passage of the 13th, 14th, and 15th amendments to the Constitution (prohibiting slavery, mandating equal due process, and giving the franchise to African Americans). During the 12-year period of Reconstruction that followed the war, Congress enacted forward-thinking legislation in the Freedmen's Bureau Act of 1866, the Civil Rights Act of 1866, the Civil Rights Act of 1870, the Civil Rights Act of 1871, and the Civil Rights Act of 1875. The so-called "Radical Republicans" responsible for enacting these ground-breaking statutes sought to fully integrate African Americans into society. But the country was not yet ready for such radical social engineering, and the Supreme Court, reflecting this popular reticence, ruled many of the Reconstruction Era laws unconstitutional, ostensibly because they infringed on state authority.

---

[11] Abraham Lincoln, Cooper Union Address in New York City, February 27, 1860. Compulsory use of politically correct speech in an effort to paper-over immorality by calling it right and normal, is not new.

The Supreme Court's regression reflected the country's willingness to end slavery, but an unwillingness to fully integrate black Americans into society during the latter part of the 19th Century. In so doing, the Federal courts unwittingly had given states the opportunity to enact America's creed, and the vision of the 14th Amendment. But the states failed this test miserably, leading in the 20th Century to a permanent decision that the Federal government, and not the states, would be the preserver of civil and human rights. During the last third of the 19th Century, the Supreme Court was more interested in legal arguments about the nature of the Federal Union than about equality of human rights.[12] When Reconstruction abruptly ended in 1877, the Federal government returned control of southern states to former confederate Democrats, whereupon so-called "Jim Crow" laws were adopted by Southerners to get around the Reconstruction-era constitutional amendments.

Jim Crow oppression of former slave populations would eventually be corrected through adoption of the 24th Amendment, the Civil Rights Act of 1964, the Voting Rights Act, and numerous Supreme Court decisions in the latter 20th Century redressing systematic discriminations that occurred for a century after Appomattox. This does not render the Constitution a hopelessly flawed document warranting it be tossed on the ash heap of history. On the contrary, it illustrates the Constitution's inherent flexibility, adaptability, and capacity for eventually correcting historical and legal errors, without losing sight of

---

[12] In *Texas v. White*, 74 U.S. (7 Wall.) 700 (1869), the Court determined secession was not allowed by the Constitution because Southern states lacked such power and legally had never left the Union. The Supreme Court in this period sought to limit, not enlarge, the application of the 14th Amendment, and rarely pushed back against Jim Crow exploitations by states. One exception to this reluctance was when some states sought to eliminate the testimony of African Americans in legal proceedings.

its original purpose (once the country's leaders finally have the stomach for change).

The unelected Supreme Court determined to not get too far ahead of what the country was willing to accept. This observation is relevant here because deferral of racial justice in the latter 19th Century eventually led to a permanent, but necessary, reduction in state sovereignty. Although they were very tardy in acting (by almost a century), the Federal government—not the states—had to step-in to extinguish "Jim Crow" laws that violated the 14th and 15th Amendments. Today, few dispute the need for these actions by the Federal government to advance the nation's ideals of liberty, equal protection under the law, and justice for all; but it nonetheless resulted in a permanent increase in Federal power. Consequently, today Federal courts are the uncontested final arbiter of civil rights and whether discriminatory practices have occurred. This necessary growth in Federal power occurred because only the Federal government could nationalize these vital amendments, and because states had abdicated their proper implementation and enforcement after the Civil War.

Though undermined in the South by Jim Crow laws, the 14th Amendment did not sit dormant in law books during the last quarter of the 19th Century. The 14th amendment was intended to guarantee freed African slaves equal protection and due process of law. Though not meant for this purpose, it was also used as a tool for applying the principles of equal protection and due process to corporations, and entities other than individual citizens. The concept of applying equal protection to banks, patent law, transportation, tariffs, and commerce was developed during this time. Using the 14th Amendment to advance the doctrine of equal protection for private corporations, the Federal government grew its power and reach by empowering business and industrial sectors—some to the point of near-monopoly. This period saw passage of the Interstate Commerce Commission Act, the Sherman Anti-Trust Act, and other laws asserting a broader and stronger role for the Federal government—not in managing the country's economy—but rather in making sure businesses all played by the same rules. From 1870 to 1900, real per capita gross national product (GNP) doubled; but not everyone shared equally in the economic growth. A small number of tycoons became very wealthy. As a result, by the early years of the 20th Century most people favored enactment of progressive income taxes so the costs of government (and Civil War military pensions) would fall to a greater extent on the wealthiest Americans. The 16th Amendment allowing taxation of income was approved by Congress in 1909 and sent to the states. Its ratification was ultimately driven by popular demands that the rich be more heavily taxed, and not by a desire to increase the taxing authority of the Federal government.

Pushback against large corporate interests did not end with enactment of the 16th Amendment. The advent of the "Progressive Era," around the start of the 20th Century, saw the Federal government transformed into an organization focused on the country's economic well-being. At the beginning of the 20th Century, helping businesses first, and the workingman second, was equated with national economic well-being by government and the citizenry. While still a candidate for Vice-President in 1900, Theodore Roosevelt adopted the language of populists and progressives in his "appeal to the workingman."[13] But Theodore Roosevelt's goal of using the Federal government to break monopoly and broaden prosperity are not found in the Constitution. Both Theodore Roosevelt and Woodrow Wilson wanted to mitigate and constrain unbridled economic power vested in a small number of private corporations. In their

---

[13] *The Streator Free Press* (Streator, Illinois), October 12, 1900, p. 6.

battles against large corporations, both presidents believed the Constitution was antiquated, did not give them the authority they needed, and that presidents should have still more, not less, power. To advance his goals, Woodrow Wilson asserted that the power of the president "is anything he has the sagacity and force to make it."[14] The Constitution's authors would have been appalled.

Before the Great Depression, the Federal government was only willing to manage the excesses of modern mercantilism by slowly increasing economic interventionism to help protect selected groups of businesses and vulnerable citizens. From the country's Gilded Age through the 1920s, it was widely believed that the country provided limitless opportunity. All that most people needed to do in order to achieve success was to work hard. That notion came to a screeching halt with the 1929 stock market crash.

The Great Depression and Franklin Delano Roosevelt's (FDR's) New Deal permanently enlarged Federal power again. In his first campaign for the White House in 1932, FDR made no secret of his preference for an unprecedented expansion in the power and reach of the Federal government. When FDR took office in 1933, America found itself in the worst economic depression ever, before or since. Millions of adults were out of work, not due to a weak work ethic or an unwillingness to work, but rather as a result of market forces entirely outside their control. Before the Great Depression, it was widely held that government should only enact regulations extending the free exercise of commerce and mitigating a few abuses. The Great Depression changed this national psyche. The presidential elections of 1932 and 1936 turned on the question of whether it was the government's job to pro-actively return the nation to

---

[14]   Lepore, p. 373.

economic prosperity through "enlightened administration" to improve the welfare of the economically displaced.

FDR believed American governance had reached a new inflection point by the 1930s: The American Frontier had been conquered, industrial robber barons had accumulated too much wealth, and equality of economic opportunity was in jeopardy to such an extent that assertive intervention by the Federal government was warranted. FDR advocated for the power of the Federal government to be realigned in radical ways not seen since the Civil War. "The task of Government," FDR said at the end of the 1932 presidential campaign, "in relation to business, is to assist the development of an economic declaration of rights, an economic constitutional order. This is the common task of statesman and businessman. It is the minimum requirement of a more permanently safe order of things."[15] FDR's new economic order was not opposed to capitalism, but it now required private businesses to partner with the government to build a large social safety net. To this end, the president believed government was justified in regulating and managing the economy with a much heavier hand.

In contrast, President Hoover believed FDR's New Deal (unemployment relief, social security, new business restrictions, regional development projects, etc.) undermined a key provision of American democracy—that people will succeed or fail principally on their own merits, and that FDR's economic interventionism would sacrifice individual liberty and freedom at the altar of government-mandated socialism.

FDR did not get all the power and constitutional realignment he sought, but he nevertheless increased the power and reach of the Federal government more than any previous president.

---

[15] Franklin Roosevelt, speech to the Commonwealth Club, San Francisco, Sept. 23, 1932.

The American people approved of Roosevelt's management of the Great Depression and World War II, despite his significant expansion of Executive and Federal power, and elected him to the White House an unprecedented four times.

In the 1930s, America searched for a different middle path—between the dictatorship and national socialism dominating Europe, and the 'hands-off' policies that led to the Great Depression. FDR's middle path lay somewhere between laissez-faire capitalism and a State-run economy. This path was not easily blazed. FDR pushed through Congress an emergency banking act, the Glass-Steagall Act, the Securities and Exchange Commission, the Agricultural Adjustment Act and later Social Security. But in 1935, the Supreme Court unanimously rejected Congress' National Recovery Administration Act because it exceeded the powers granted to Congress in the Constitution's commerce clause. In 1936, eight more Acts of Congress intended to provide Depression relief were struck down—leading FDR to try (unsuccessfully) to pack the court. In the end, a new Congress, the President, and the Supreme Court ultimately found a new balance when FDR was able to replace a few high court justices, and Congress modified its methods of providing Depression relief, with the result that new assistance and reform bills were upheld by the Supreme Court. Once again, a constitutional compromise in the national interest led to an expansion of Federal power.

In the 1930s, new powers wielded by the Federal Executive Branch were not bolstered by new constitutional revisions—they were purely the product of political compromise and altered views of the Constitution. Civil rights and anti-discrimination policies, by contrast, had been supported by post-Civil War constitutional amendments, much later by the 24th Amendment, and by key court decisions like *Brown v. Board of Education*

(1954). FDR's Depression-driven growth in Federal power during the 1930s (and later increases in Federal power during the last half of the 20th Century) were mostly the product of political accommodation and compromise, not constitutional revision and landmark Supreme Court decisions.

The New Deal rejected the notion that capitalism should be unbridled, and it began a long arc of Liberalism and expansion of Federal power stretching from FDR's second inaugural in 1937, through World War Two, and into the latter years of the Lyndon Johnson Administration when the Viet Nam War overwhelmed domestic politics. Until the late 1960s, Americans largely supported expansions of Federal power. These expansions produced the Great Society, the War on Poverty, the Civil Rights Act of 1964, Interstate highways, the Voting Rights Act, a landmark education act, added Medicare to Social Security and led to passage of the Law Enforcement Assistance Administration Act. These policy changes were not primarily intended to increase the powers of the Federal government (though they did), but instead to achieve broadly popular policy outcomes. Despite their popularity, words of warning were always part of the debate. Herbert Hoover outlived FDR by almost two decades; he and others continued to argue that government "founded on the coercion and compulsory organization of men" would result in a loss of liberty and freedom.[16]

Later still in the 20th Century, the Federal government asserted new powers over the economy in labor law, environmental protection, transportation regulations, special rights for the handicapped, and other subjects of legislation remaining in place today—always without constitutional amendment. Most citizens supported these policies and were largely unaware of how they

[16] Herbert Hoover, speech in Denver, Colorado, October 30, 1936.

gradually compounded an imbalance in American federalism and in the relationship between state and national governments.

In 1964, Ronald Reagan started asking whether "we believe in our capacity for self-government or whether we [should] abandon the American Revolution and confess that a little intellectual elite in a far distant capital can plan our lives for us better than we can plan ourselves." It was one of several early indicators that the Federal government had become too large and too powerful—and that the Constitution's balance-of-power was out of balance. Nonetheless, the size and scope of the Federal government continued to grow.

The Nixon presidency brought a different kind of change. His term in office saw a string of reports about how the war in Viet Nam was prosecuted, including the release of the Pentagon Papers in 1971. These documents not only characterized how Administrations prior to President Nixon's had bungled the Viet Nam War, they demonstrated to the entire country that the Federal government could not be trusted. This message was reinforced a few years later by Watergate and the resignation of the president for lying and obstruction of justice. Too much power led to abuses of power. By the 1970s and 1980s, not only was the Federal government seen as untrustworthy, but the Federal/State relationship had been turned upside down by aggressive Federal use of "power-of-the-purse" to enforce legislative actions that were not among Congress' enumerated powers (e.g., speed limits, drinking ages, etc.). It happened gradually, but in the space of less than a century, the "necessary and proper" clause had neutered the 10th Amendment and States were now required to serve the governance objectives of the Federal government, rather than the other way around.

It took several years for the 1973 *Roe v. Wade* decision to become a part of the Federal over-reach argument, but by the late

1990s, it was clear the Constitution contained no right to privacy; that the Supreme Court's creation of a privacy doctrine based on the *Griswold v. Connecticut* case (allowing married couples to make their own private birth control decisions without government intervention) could not provide legal cover for killing unborn children. With *Roe v. Wade* the Supreme Court was legislating from the bench. Again, the Federal government had gone too far. Forty-nine years later, the *Dobbs v. Jackson* (2022) case affirmed that the Supreme Court should not legislate, and that abortion policy was a matter properly left to legislatures, not courts.

Also beginning in the 1970s, the Equal Rights Amendment sputtered and failed. Phyllis Schlafly has been blamed for sinking the ERA, but this gives her too much credit. Schlafly simply gave voice to a view that resonated with a population grown suspicious of the central government. If adopted, Schlafly claimed, the Federal government would use the ERA to create federally mandated gender-neutral bathrooms, federally mandated same-sex marriage, federally mandated integration of women into combat roles, and the systematic repeal of privileges women then enjoyed under the law (by way of courts, the Federal government made these changes anyway, despite the ERA's failure). Whatever the ERA's merits, its rejection reflected, in part, reluctance, suspicion, and a growing weariness over the Federal government's never-ending expansion of power, their assumption of powers not enumerated in the Constitution, their willingness to use the court system to advance ever more Federal power accumulation, and the adoption of policies pushed by special interests that could not be enacted legislatively (and likely violated the original intent of the 9th and 10th Amendments).

President Reagan's brand of conservatism may have briefly slowed the growth of the Federal government, but it did not last. Responses to the September 11, 2001 terrorist attacks in the form of the Patriot Act, the partial nationalization of education policy in "No Child Left Behind" laws, the Federal response to Hurricane Katrina, and other Federal policies, collectively propelled an otherwise conservative George W. Bush Administration toward significant enlargement of Federal power. Expansion of Federal power continued under the Obama and Biden Administrations. The corresponding erosion of state and local authority in a nation with a unique heritage of decentralized federalism changed the face of the nation. Both parties acted to grow the Federal government. When Democrats dominated Congress and the White House for all but eight years between 1933 and 1969, Republicans decried the expansion of presidential power. But when Republicans controlled the White House for 20 of the 24 years between 1969 and 1993, they also came to favor expanded Federal and presidential powers. In the 21st Century, there is no appreciable difference between the two major parties' love for the exercise of broad Federal power—the only difference lies in their policy objectives. It is no coincidence, therefore, that between 1958 and 2015 the percentage of Americans who told pollsters that they "basically trusted the government" fell from 73% to 19%.[17]

Another statistical indicator of Federal power accumulation concerns the number of executive orders issued by presidents. Only after 1900 does the annual rate of executive orders issued by the president pass 100. It stays above 100 per year throughout the presidencies of Republicans and Democrats (from Theodore Roosevelt to Harry Truman), and then decreases to an average of 56 per year from Dwight Eisenhower to Donald Trump. President Biden's rate of executive order issuance will take the annual number well over 100 for the first time in 70 years.[18]

---

[17] Lepore, p. 726.
[18] Statistics of The American Presidency Project, University of California Santa Barbara, 2021.

Federal power is no longer balanced if the president rules by fiat and decree.

As the Federal government increased its size and reach, Congress authorized the creation of various regulatory agencies, positioned under the Executive Branch, to implement Congress' laws, oversee their enactment, and create regulations compatible with the original intentions of Congress. This produced a long list of alphabet-soup agencies: the EPA, FEC, FTC, FCC, SEC, and others, who now write many new laws (called administrative regulations) that are not approved by Congress. It was never intended for regulatory agencies to be used by the Executive Branch to enact completely new laws and policies without Congressional approval. Such actions disrupt the constitutional 'balance of power' by giving potentially dictatorial legislative powers to the Executive Branch when these powers constitutionally belong to the Congress.

"Originalism" (ascertaining the intent of the Constitution's framers as a primary guide for settling legal disputes) as a movement is also a reaction to deep mistrust in government, and a reaction to unchecked growth in Federal power. Liberals assert Originalism is just a modern invention of the Pro-Life movement and/or 2nd Amendment advocates. But Originalism existed long before these modern policy movements—just under different names. Supreme Court opinions are replete with references to what the original Framers intended throughout the history of the Court. Originalism is supported in part by a lesser of two evils argument: given the choice between leaving court justices to decide cases and modernize constitutional law based on: 1) their own changing world views, on one hand, and 2) trying to figure out what the Framers meant, on the other hand—Originalism is philosophically more consistent, and is the lesser evil because it uses a common point-of-reference, and it does not forever freeze 18th Century interpretations anyway since the Constitution can always be amended. Liberal constitutional interpretations (option #1) are more likely based on shifting views; Originalism (option #2) is more fixed, and generally less susceptible to change; but when it is needed, the Constitution can still be changed via its amendment processes.

When Liberalism's power to achieve its objectives through expanded executive power and the accumulation of programmatic authority in Washington peaked in the early 1970s, Liberal elites turned to judicial remedies to increase Federal power. It has taken conservatives 50 years to stem this activist judicial strategy. Originalism was not invented by the political Right, but it has certainly been used by the Right to advance their partisan goals. Accordingly, Originalism is now used as a criterion for judicial selection by the Right and for advancing potential jurists for appointment based on Originalist opinions. After so many years Liberal Neo-Federalism remains baked into modern governance and firmly embedded in constitutional law—though it is not embedded in the Constitution itself. Liberal Neo-Federalism cannot be easily reconciled with Originalism, and a few Acts of Congress or a change in the occupant of the White House will not result in political or philosophical realignments regarding the proper role of the judiciary in shaping government policy. Any hope of resolving this deeply partisan divide requires a remedy springing from the Constitution itself—one formed through compromise, consensus, and amendment, perhaps via a convention of states.

Hopefully, delegates to a modern 'convention of states' will be thoughtful and deliberative as they evaluate possible constitutional amendments intended to modernize the Constitution and create a more balanced system of federalism for the 21st Century and beyond. States were never intended to be satellite outposts of, and their governors were not intended to be branch managers for, the Federal government. Most of the daily work of governance was intentionally left to the states by the Constitution. Founding Fathers deliberately gave a finite list of powers to the Federal government, reserving all other powers to States and The People (via Article Four, and the 9th and 10th Amendments to the Constitution). Over the years, Federal courts have had to step in and make sure state-level decisions were made in a manner that protected civil rights and equal due process for all; but the principle of separate plenary powers is still valid (though unappreciated). The purposes of the 9th and 10th amendments have been diluted and largely forgotten in the 21st Century. These last provisions of the Bill of Rights became victims of deference to the "necessary and proper" and the "general welfare" clauses of the Constitution, and of national leaders willing to forgo constitutional balance in exchange for more Federal power. A convention of states could re-establish a new 'balance of power' structure while still affirming a broader role for the Federal government.

The Founding Fathers knew they were creating an experimental government. It remains an ongoing experiment. States should be allowed to test new policies and programs. Their successes will likely be replicated in other states; their failures will impact only a few states rather than the entire country. Except where the Constitution expressly gives power to the Federal government to intervene, the national government should respect plenary and original powers of State governments and should negotiate with states over other powers. If authority heretofore exercised at the state level should be shifted to the Federal level (or vice versa), this should be negotiated by participants in ways that maintain the principles of balanced power. It is not the job of the central government to use its vast powers to homogenize the country by force.

The Federal government should always act to maintain the Union, assert the rule of law and equality of opportunity; but there is a limit to how much new power can be accumulated at the national level before admonitions of past leaders about the degradation of individual freedoms and liberty are seen to be accurate. If state governments are just places on a map, with no remaining plenary powers and autonomy of their own to balance and check the authoritarian tendencies of a central government, then the Constitution is not just out-of-balance, it has been breached and hijacked.

Chapter Three

Convening & Managing a Second Constitutional Convention

How can a nation so divided by partisanship ever hope to peacefully conduct an Article Five convention of states? If the divisive and deeply partisan rhetoric of modern political debate comes to characterize the deliberations of a Second Constitutional Convention, its work product will be scarred and damaged before it is ever submitted to states for ratification. Recommendations emerging from a fractured and nakedly partisan convention will be "damaged goods" with little chance of securing ratification from 38 states. For proposals to succeed and advance to ratification will require near-consensus coming out of the convention. Overcoming legal and procedural hurdles just to arrive at the convention's opening session will prove daunting. Once a convention is actually convened, attendees will find no rules in place for managing the convention. Before and during a convention of states, partisans will seek to manipulate Congressional, state legislative, and/or court instructions to advance their own political goals. Chaos is a distinct risk, and there is a real possibility that a second constitutional convention disbands in frustration with no amendments sent to states.

Some factions will deliberately seek to create chaos because they would prefer to leave the existing constitutional system alone, and/or create more national division. Members of Congress could be among this group, as some amendments might restrain the power and prerogatives of Congress by giving more power to states and The People. If chaos ensues at the convention, the American people will rightly wonder if there is any practical and peaceful way to resolve thorny, partisan and controversial matters of governance deferred for generations. But all these barriers and obstacles can be overcome, if there is sufficient advance planning, collaboration, and compromise.

The 'before, during, and after' logistics of a Second Constitutional Convention must be thought through carefully. Poor planning, leading to dysfunction and mismanagement at the convention, will give openings for more polarization, extremism and division, and then this unique Sestercentennial opportunity for governance enhancement will be lost to history. To be successful, planning for the 'before, during, and after' of constitutional convention logistics needs to revolve around five key questions:

A. How can the country navigate the uncharted territory between when 34 states have called for a convention and when it is initially gaveled to order?

B. What should be the role of Congress (and/or the Supreme Court) in setting the agenda, selecting delegates, and making other rules for officiating a convention of states?

C. How can the convention maintain a civil dialogue when passions and partisanship sharply divide many of its members and sessions?

D. Once the convention is gaveled to order, what meeting management protocols and formal process rules should be employed to guide and organize the convention?

E. How should proposed amendments be presented to states and citizens after they are approved by the convention?

* * * * *

A. How can the country navigate the uncharted territory between when 34 states have called for a convention and when it is gaveled to order?

Once it has been determined that the requisite number of states have called for a convention, it must be held. The Constitution does not allow Congress to ignore a lawfully summoned convention of states, if at least 34 state applications are valid and contemporary. The role of Congress is purely ministerial; they "shall call a convention for proposing amendments" if requested by at least 34 states. Nonetheless, there will be political mischief and intrigue, and it will likely center around whether the applications are valid and contemporary. The words "valid" and "contemporary" do not appear in Article Five, so litigation is likely. Litigation may find final resolution only at the U.S. Supreme Court, and there are no legal precedents regarding the calling of Article Five conventions.

Nor is there a legal mechanism for compelling Congress to do its duty to call an Article Five convention, if they resist. Remedies would be limited to political pressure, media hype and various legal actions. The American people will have the task of cutting through the haze of competing propaganda and dire predictions from those who believe the country will collapse into undemocratic chaos if a Second Constitutional Convention is convened. Amid the fog created by convention opponents, and claims that democracy will be undermined, three principal questions need to be resolved:

1. <u>What legally constitutes a constitutionally correct call for a convention of states?</u> The language of Article Five requires that a convention be held upon "the Application of the Legislatures of two-thirds of the several States . . . for proposing Amendments." The word "Legislatures" means governors have no formal vote or veto, and it means each state's convention call should reflect action by the entire legislature, not just one house. What constitutes an "application" should be liberally construed. Absent specific limitations in the language of Article Five, courts should not invent restrictions they think might be hiding between the lines of Article Five requiring 34 or more applications to be identical. States that have already submitted applications for a convention have done so by approving joint resolutions, adopted by both houses of the state legislature. Minor variations in form, or different amendment topics offered by different states, are insufficient grounds for preventing a convention of states. If, generally speaking, 34 states have formally expressed their desire to Congress for a convention of states "for proposing amendments," even if for differing topics, and at least 34 of the applications are reasonably current (contemporary), then this would constitute the threshold the Framers had in mind. It would then be an expression of The People and the States that the time has come for constitutional revisions to be debated via a convention of states.

2. <u>Can the convention of states' agenda be effectively limited to one or more delineated subjects in advance?</u> This will be a key consideration in efforts to secure convention applications

from 34 states because some states will want limits on the convention's deliberations. The answer is probably 'yes and no,' and under the circumstances, this answer should suffice.

All states that have already adopted joint resolutions calling for a convention of states list specific amendment topics that led them to make the convention call in the first place. Due to the efforts of the conservative leaning Convention of States Action Project, recent state resolutions look remarkably similar. Some state resolutions may say they only want revisions dealing with topics listed in their resolutions. But Article Five contains no language allowing individual states to limit the agenda of a convention of states.

Congress may attempt to limit the agenda via their constitutional responsibility to "call" the convention, but they can only make official suggestions. Convention delegates will likely give considerable deference to Congress' recommendations, and to instructions from states. But it is unlikely that State and Congressional instructions could legally constrain convention delegates from discussing whatever amendments and topics they wish. Furthermore, a revision to one section of the Constitution could require or trigger changes in another section to avoid inconsistency. The language of Article Five, and commentaries about it provided by its original authors, suggest that if 34 states generally believe the language of the Constitution needs amending, even without specifics, the convention may act as their collective conscience leads. But in the current political environment, amendment proposals straying too far from Congressional and State instructions will face greater resistance in the convention, and later during ratification.

If delegates are appointed by states, they could theoretically be recalled if a state believes they are acting beyond the scope of their instructions. Some states, in their resolutions calling for a convention, provide for such recalls. If delegates are popularly elected, they will likely campaign based on the topics they will, and will not, advance—thus providing a political, if not legal, mechanism for limiting the agenda. In an extreme situation, if the convention ventures too far from acceptable agenda topics, some delegates would likely withdraw, which could threaten quorums and subsequent ratification efforts. A convention of states cannot compel attendance by delegates. Many delegates appointed to the original Constitutional Convention in 1787 did not attend all or significant portions of the sessions. For this reason, quorum rules set by a modern convention of states will be an important first step in determining how amendments are adopted and sent on to the states. In the main, however, convention delegates will need to reach final decisions by near consensus to have any expectation of success when state-by-state ratifications begin. There are not 38 Blue states, nor 38 Red states. Recommended amendments will have to have bipartisan support to succeed.

3. Can state resolutions calling for a convention of states that were subsequently rescinded by the same states be excluded from the count in determining if 34 states have lawfully called for a Second Constitutional Convention, and when do state calls expire? Since the provisions of Article Five have never been used, there is no case law or precedent available to answer this question. Some states have rescinded previous actions by their legislatures approving the ERA, as well as calls for a convention of

states. The calling of a convention of states should reflect a national mood that the Constitution requires some degree of revision and amendment—at roughly the same point in time. The use of resolutions issued by states in earlier centuries for different purposes would be perceived as exploitation of a loophole to get around the practical intent of Article Five.

This is not a purely hypothetical problem; some state calls for a convention of states are from a different era and century and lack expiration dates. Though unexpired, they should not reasonably be considered to be either current or contemporary. If the 34+ state calls are not all reasonably contemporary (from the 21st Century), any convention would be without effective mandate, and this would erode its legitimacy. Rescinding a previous resolution calling for a convention of states is a clear signal that a state does not believe this remains an appropriate course of action; and this decision should be respected.

Many (but not all) recent state resolutions requesting a convention of states specifically say their calls for a second convention will expire if no convention is called by a certain date. Calls for a convention of states should represent the aggregate and current intentions of the states. This approach is compatible with recent decisions properly rejecting efforts to achieve a tardy ratification of the Equal Rights Amendment (ERA) by counting as approvals state decisions that were later rescinded, and those that ignore congressionally adopted ERA ratification deadlines that came and went long ago.

In January 2022, Nebraska adopted a convention of states resolution. Nebraska's document[19] calls for amendments to enact Congressional term limits, limit the size and scope of the Federal government, and create fiscal restraints on the central government (without details as to the exact nature of such fiscal restraints or exact language limiting the size of government). If a convention of states is called, it is reasonable to assume Nebraska's delegates will see these three topics as their chief mandate; and if Nebraska officials appoint their convention delegates, then they will likely name representatives committed to honoring these amendment priorities. If Nebraska's delegates are popularly elected, they may or may not feel constrained to follow their legislature's instructions.

States may pass convention resolutions containing only broad directions, while others may be more specific. Nebraska's convention resolution is not identical to those passed by other states; but it is strikingly similar to a model resolution developed by the Convention of States Project. Actual state resolutions differ, but what almost all have in common is language taken directly from, and in compliance with, Article Five to "call a Convention for proposing Amendments."

The media, States and the public will have to trust convention delegates to act prudently and in good faith as they address uncertainties that cannot be entirely known before the convention starts. If the convention's work product is unacceptable it will be rejected during the ratification process.

---

[19] LR14 was passed by the Nebraska Legislature on January 28, 2022. The entire Nebraska resolution is included in the appendix. It calls for a convention "limited to proposing amendments" to the Constitution and lists these 3 amendment topics. Nebraska's convention call expires on February 1, 2027.

B. What should be the role of Congress (and/or the Supreme Court, if necessary) in setting the agenda, selecting delegates, and other rules for a convention of states?

Presumably, as part of its ministerial duties, Congress can name the time, place and expiration date of the convention. Can they name the presiding officer? Can they set the agenda? Can they prescribe a system for appointing or electing delegates? Must Congress fund the convention? These questions may produce more litigation (chiefly intended to thwart a convention). Much should be left to convention delegates to decide for themselves. In the midst of more legal and political maneuvering, however, these are the most pertinent questions to be resolved regarding the role of Congress:

1. Who should serve as leader and presiding officer(s) of the convention? The convention's leadership will be key to its success. If its leaders are overtly partisan, it will de-legitimize amendment recommendations. For its initial sessions, the Congressional "call" for a convention could name the Vice-President or the Chief Justice of the Supreme Court as interim presiding officer; but ultimately, the convention needs to select its own leaders, and they must be respected by all factions, Right and Left leaning, and be persons able to act as bridges between partisans, able to embrace the intrinsic value of consensus and compromise. In 1787, this person was George Washington. Many of the delegates already realized Washington would likely be the country's first president; he embodied the national spirit, and he had the gravitas to compel compromise between Federalists and Anti-Federalists based on his national standing and accomplishments.

2. How shall delegates to the convention be selected? Delegates could be appointed by each state or elected by Congressional District, or through some other method. The first constitutional convention allowed five to seven representatives per state, regardless of whether each delegation represented a populous or sparsely inhabited state. It was up to each state to appoint their delegates, and the leadership of the convention had little choice but to wait for a quorum of members to straggle into Philadelphia with appointment papers from their state leaders to begin formal debates because they lacked legal mechanisms to compel attendance.

Modern convention delegates should read the proceedings of the First Constitutional Convention; but a Second Constitutional Convention will not be bound by practices of the first. If it was, the conclave could include 200 to 400 delegates from all 50 states (a manageable assembly). Congress' authority to call a convention of states could be construed to include instructions on whether delegates will be elected or appointed—although some recent state convention applications attempt to assert a state's prerogative in determining how their delegates are selected. In devising a method for delegate selection, Congress must settle on a process that will assemble delegates perceived by the general population as reasonably representative of the nation's moods concerning constitutional reform.

Over the last century, the United States has gradually embedded the principle of "one-man-one-vote" into the election of democratic representatives and the construction of its public assemblies, even though this principle does not apply to the U.S. Senate or to the process of ratifying constitutional amendments. With these exceptions, "one-man-one-vote" is established law. The country would likely demand an equivalent delegate selection system, based on population; without it, the convention's legitimacy and public standing could be undermined before it started. If Congress asserted a proportional representative system for electing or appointing delegates, it likely would not be contested because Article Five does not prescribe any competing method, because devising a delegate selection method can reasonably be argued as falling within the scope of Congress' convention "call," and because it would be based on accepted "one-man-one-vote" principles. Congress' call should also include a process for verifying the eligibility of delegates before they are seated—presumably with affidavits issued by each state certifying their appointment or popular election.

3. <u>How shall a convention be funded and empowered</u>? This could also be addressed in Congress' call for the convention. The Congressional call should provide for compensation and living arrangements for each delegate—comparable to what is provided to Members of Congress. Congress should also provide funds for staff support, and give delegates limited powers to call witnesses and experts to aid them in their deliberations. But a convention of states should not function at the mercy of Congress. If Congress refuses to support the convention, each state should expect to contribute funding in proportion to its representation.

4. <u>To what extent can Congress set and limit the convention's agenda</u>? Congress must "call" the convention, but since applications were brought by the states, and since Article Five was provided in the first place as a mechanism for

working around a resistive Congress, it seems reasonable that Congress should not control the agenda. The Congress of Confederation broadly charged delegates in 1787 with re-writing the Articles of Confederation, under which the United States government had operated since 1781. But many Constitutional Convention delegates believed then that an entirely new structure of government should be proposed to replace the Articles of Confederation. Most of these delegates recognized that the United States needed a new government, rather than a system to hold together semi-autonomous states for purposes of winning a war.

A second constitutional convention will operate within a completely different context. In 1787, the Congress of Confederation could have decided to veto the work of the First Constitutional Convention. But they realized there was not support for the system then in use, so they sent the new scheme to the states. A second constitutional convention will send their recommendations directly to states. There is no broad support today for complete abolition of the current Constitution. In the unlikely event a 21st Century convention of states began with debate over whether they should amend the existing document or propose an entirely new one, the latter option would not have majority support.

The possibility of a complete replacement of the existing Constitution is what gives opponents of a modern convention of states their greatest fears. Such fear is unwarranted. As mentioned above, most states today will try to constrain delegates to consider only certain topics, which will keep the convention focused on a narrower agenda and on targeted amendments and revisions to the existing Constitution—not its replacement.

In fact, there will likely be some delegates who oppose *any* amendments due to their fidelity to the original Constitution. Congressional recommendations for amendments will carry weight, but Congress will have no legal mechanism to restrict the convention's agenda; Congress' suggestions should reflect salient topics and instructions from state applications; but that is all. Anything else would be overreach by Congress.

C. How can the convention maintain a civil dialogue when passions and partisanship will sharply divide many of its members and sessions?

Controlling and taming partisan bickering will pose a huge challenge. The First Constitutional Convention met in Philadelphia without agreement on any key principles of governance. From May to July in 1787, the convention hotly debated the 15 points of Madison's Virginia Plan, but reached no consensus. Nonetheless, this extended debate produced in the minds of many delegates a broad idea of what a new government should look like and where delegates would likely find agreement from a sizeable majority of participants. By July 1787, a 'Committee of Detail' was appointed to draft what the majority of delegates likely believed should comprise the rough framework for a new government. The document created by the Committee of Detail underwent numerous revisions after it was reported back to the full convention; it was, arguably, the first draft of the U.S. Constitution. In the same manner, an extended period of debate and deliberation could occupy the initial months of a Second Constitutional Convention to determine the collective views of delegates—before specific amendment proposals are advanced, sorted, and assigned to committees. In the current political environment, however, extended debate fueled by polarized media coverage could act as a barrier to compromise rather than a facilitator of compromise. The initial weeks of a second convention of states should not produce quick amendment proposals; but it will signal whether future compromise will be hard to achieve.

While there is no way to guarantee toxic partisanship does not overwhelm a second constitutional convention, there are a few practical steps that can be taken to mitigate the impacts of polarizing political rancor. These include:

1. <u>Adopt a Code of Ethics for the Convention</u>. Governments at all levels have adopted "Code of Ethics" documents to encourage good behavior. There are several existing governmental ethics codes to use as a template. For example, the Georgia Code of Ethics for public officials contains ten provisions, listed using Roman numerals in the fashion of an older, better known law code.[20] Whatever its form, a code of ethics for the convention should be adopted and vigorously enforced. It should prohibit personal attacks and incendiary vitriol in open sessions, just as Congressional rules prohibit the same coarse behavior now. It should also extend to external statements outside the convention. If delegates are required to be civil only during regular sessions of the convention, and then tear each other to shreds on Twitter and Sunday afternoon television talk shows, simple politeness during formal meetings will not be enough, and the work of the convention will suffer. Violations of the adopted code of ethics should be dealt with quickly and include expulsion for the most egregious misbehaviors—because the stakes are too great and retaining

---

[20] Official Code of Georgia Annotated (OCGA), 45-10-1

the people's trust in the process too important. Such a code of ethics may even rekindle an interest in public and private morality and the recognition that government leaders must have both.

2.   Agree on Common Governance Reference Points. While a code of ethics is useful for regulating public and private conduct and keeping tempers in check, whether delegates to a Second Constitutional Convention adopt such a code may be less important than adopting a Charter of Government Principles. If convention delegates differ too much on the essential roles and basic purposes of government, they are unlikely to agree on amendments. Before delegates get down to the business of deciding how to amend the Constitution, they need to take time to find common ground on fundamental questions concerning the role of government in the 21st Century—in what activities government should, and should not, be engaged and whether there should be stricter limits (on which most delegates can agree) for containing the reach of government. The convention should craft a Charter of Governance Principles with the understanding it will be used not just to write amendments compatible with the Charter, but also as a treatise for guiding policy decisions of local, state, and Federal governments in the future, thereby helping the nation redefine what "balanced" and "limited government" means in the 21st Century. Madison's Virginia Plan was not adopted in 1787; but debate over the plan's merits and weaknesses was a mechanism for getting delegates to think about governance principles they could agree upon—and these eventually evolved into the Constitution.

Some of the factions that will form in a modern convention of states will look like ones from the 1787 convention (e.g., national versus state driven federalism; should or shouldn't the powers of the Federal government be strictly limited to enumerated topics; should national taxing powers be expanded or constrained; how should the president be selected?, etc.), while other factions will coalesce around new issues (e.g., should there be constitutional limitations on Big Tech's ability to restrict free speech; should matters of immigration and control of the border be the subject of constitutional amendment; should the Federal government's "power-of-the-purse" be constrained; etc.). Fundamental differences about the role of government in the modern world could paralyze the convention just as it paralyzes Congress today. For this reason, proactive strategies to find consensus around the role and functions of the Federal and state governments are required. Early agreement on these basic or "first governance" principles may be a key strategy for finding compromise and common ground in the subsequent drafting of amendments. It won't eliminate partisanship and polarization, but it could, at a minimum, make the arguments manageable.

The Trump and Biden administrations have amply demonstrated that intense partisan bickering, character assassination, and political bludgeoning are not effective in producing compromise or in drafting policies commanding a broad base of support. Trump and Biden Era partisanship has only produced deadlock and public disdain. Today, Congress seems content with partisan deadlock. But a convention of states will have a limited shelf-life and will exist for only one purpose: producing proposed amendments.

Delegates will not want to be known after the convention for failing to achieve their objectives. To be successful, they will have to seek out compromises with the greatest chance of securing ratification by the states. Article Five may be a creature of the 18th Century, but its functional insistence on compromise may pull 21st Century America back from the brink of partisan self-destruction.

The writing of a "Charter of Governance Principles" that establishes new parameters around the role of government, and therefore, the scope and reach of constitutional amendments, will also be a difficult exercise. This debate will reverberate with the diverse views of participating delegates. But without common governance reference points, there is little possibility of reaching agreement on how to amend the Constitution—the document upon which the rest of American governance is based. For this reason, what follows are a few key topics and principles to discuss and then incorporate into a Charter of Governance Principles, all in the interests of creating common reference points.

2.a. **Define the terms "limited government" and "co-equal" branches**. The Constitution gives more power to Congress than to any other branch of government; but the Framers still sought to limit excessive accumulation of power and the abuse of power by any single branch. Each branch acts independent of the other, to a point. The executive branch checks the legislative branch through limited veto powers, the power to pardon, make appointments, and in its role as the head of the military. The legislative branch checks the executive branch through its impeachment power, exclusive power to levy taxes, approve treaties and key appointments, and enact all new laws. The judicial branch can determine the constitutionality of laws, but the president appoints the Federal judiciary, and the legislature can impeach judges and justices, and so forth. This interlocking architecture of government remains "limited" only if every branch retains sufficient independence to restrain tyrannical tendencies from taking hold in one or both of the other branches. If tyranny and unchecked dictatorial actions cannot be reined-in, then the architecture of government is no longer balanced and the branches no longer co-equal. For this reason, Congress cannot, and should not, permanently delegate its power to make new laws, new policies and the levying of new taxes to bureaucrats in the Executive Branch.

2.b. **Separation of Church and State**. A large majority of Americans still believe in a higher power. Since humans cannot alter natural laws, it is reasonable for the nation to permit some deference to the Creator of natural law. Natural laws and many human behaviors, however, do not require codification, regulation, or criminalization. Some are matters of individual conscience and common sense lying outside the scope of government. Some people believe government rests on Christ's shoulders, while others believe it is the other way around.[21] Either way, government and religion need to respect each other's space. Religion does not need, nor should it anticipate, the government's help; it just needs government to stay in its lane. Likewise, government should expect religious organizations to stay in their lane. Governments should not tell people how to think, how to worship,

---

[21] Isaiah 9:6-7; Matthew 22:21.

what values they want instilled in children, or that the natural order of the universe is not what it appears to be. If the First Amendment is not sufficiently clear, and the philosophical underpinnings of 'separation of church and state' need revision in the 21st Century, then this should be hashed out in advance with the results embedded in a Charter of Governance Principles.

2.c. **Define the basic purposes of government and whether there should be limitations on the reach and scope of government in the Constitution.** Government was not ordained to dominate and control all aspects of human existence. Government should benefit the people by assuring their safety and security; and government should serve the people, not the other way around. Government should encourage creative and commercial genius to flourish, but not at the expense of the environment, the poor, the vulnerable, or the elderly. Regardless the country's economic system, it is the responsibility of the government to provide, by some means, for the protection of persons who are less fortunate, to assure the environment remains livable, and that equality of opportunity (and reasonable access to the same) is maintained. Government should intervene when natural avarice threatens to create harmful imbalances, and it should do so within its financial means. It should ensure equal opportunity and due process for all, and it should protect citizens from the unintended consequences of economic and cultural disruptions and natural disaster. How government charts this course, circumscribes its proper role, and determines those aspects of human life that should remain OUTSIDE the domain of government, warrant explanation in a Charter of Governance Principles.

2.d. **Does the Constitution need an updated version of "The Great Compromise?"** If so, what are its principal tenets? The convention will likely determine that there should be a greater role for the Federal government in the 21ˢᵗ Century than was necessary in the 18ᵗʰ Century; but such a decision does not mean structural balances and checks cannot be retained to keep state and Federal levels of government more effectively balanced.

The "enumeration" (specific listing) of Federal powers in the Constitution, and the delegation of most other functions and powers to the states, was intentionally designed to create balanced federalism with plenary and original powers given to *both* the national and state governments. The Framers did not design a pure majoritarian democracy. They intended deference be given to unique state and regional views. They never intended states and regions to always be subservient to a national majority, especially with slim majorities likely to switch at the next election. Political compromise and consensus are superior to tyrannical majoritarianism. Compromise and consensus keep factions in check. The interests of the majority should not be ignored, but nor should state and regional interests. The Great Compromise of 1787 was the 18ᵗʰ Century solution for this dilemma. A new 21ˢᵗ Century great compromise solution may be required to bridge the rural-urban divide. The philosophical assumptions of a 21ˢᵗ Century Great Compromise (if one is required in the first place) should be included in a new Charter of Governance Principles. Failing to address this issue in a second constitutional convention will create a potent barrier to success.

2.e. **Solving the problems of gun violence requires a common constitutional reference point if current divisions over the meaning of the Second Amendment are to be overcome.** The Second Amendment is here to stay, and guns should not be outlawed; but it is in the national interest to keep guns away from certain members of society who will abuse the privileges of the Second Amendment. How can this be accomplished? Some believe the Second Amendment was rendered antiquated by the creation of a permanent standing army. By contrast, the *D.C. v. Heller* (2008) and *McDonald v. Chicago* (2010) Supreme Court cases interpreted the Second Amendment as endowing a permanent individual right to possess firearms. Others believe the Second Amendment can be interpreted to allow states to restrict gun access to citizen militias—whatever that might look like in the 21ˢᵗ Century.[22] This is discussed in greater detail below, and again in Chapter Four; but a Charter of Governance Principles needs to find common ground on the matter of gun control or no Second Amendment revisions will ever see ratification.

2.f. **Free Speech.** Convention delegates should take time to re-affirm their commitment to the basic tenets of the First Amendment and contemplate how new speech platforms have changed (as well as what Americans

---

[22] For a modern description of different Second Amendment legal theories see: Cooling, Anthony D., *Still a Hollow Hope: State Power and the Second Amendment*, Ann Arbor, University of Michigan Press, 2022.

think about traditional free speech doctrines) in a Charter of Governance Principles. The convention could say: "Freedom of speech, freedom of religion, freedom of assembly, freedom of thought, and freedom of association are sacred rights, and no governmental or non-governmental entity operating in the public square should infringe upon them without demonstrating a clear and present danger to life and property." Cancelling unpopular views may also be a right of free speech, but this practice too should have limitations. Hopefully convention delegates can at least agree that indoctrinating students and minors and failing to encourage independent thought are Soviet-style control tactics with no place in America.

Whatever comprises a "Charter of Governance Principles" for use by a convention of states to guide amendment deliberations, such a treatise will surely depart from the few suggested topics above. Whatever the document looks like, it should be crafted with the goal of assisting delegates to find common ground about the roles and functions of government. This necessary first step for a second constitutional convention will be highly contentious; but based on the temperature of modern political partisanship, it is long overdue. Successfully reconciling intense rivalries to find compromise and consensus usually starts with finding common ground on key principles and concepts.

Seeking compromise and consensus in the interests of uniting divergent factions is hard work. Because it will be difficult, many people may choose instead to talk *past* their political opponents rather than *with* them. For example, Second Amendment gun enthusiasts assert as their paramount first principle that gun ownership is a basic human right. Gun control activists assert as their paramount first principle that restricting gun ownership generally is the best way to keep criminals and the mentally ill from readily obtaining firearms. As long as one group defines the issue as a civil right, and the other side defines the issue as a public necessity, there will be no common point of reference. How can these divided sides find common ground? Perhaps by agreeing upon the conditions where gun ownership should not be permitted, and when citizens can be trusted with firearms, embodied in constitutional amendments that Founding Fathers would have favored as well. If delegates to a convention of states can find a common point of reference for effective governance on an issue as intractable as gun control, then imagine how much easier it might be to find common reference points on issues like balance of power, states' rights, election regulation, laws to oversee Big Tech's influence over free speech, budgetary and fiscal discipline, and other constitutional matters.

Taking months to agree on common governance principles may frustrate an electorate accustomed to seeing action immediately following the "tip off" of sporting events; but early discussions on principle, and then building strategies for compromise, will ease the struggle when contentious debates over procedure, convention rules, and amendments arise. To the extent the general public, via the media, becomes involved in this process, it could even lead to a new public discussion about governance with lasting value for a population insufficiently schooled in basic civics.

D. Once the convention is gaveled to order, what meeting management protocols and formal rules should be used to advance the work of the convention?

The constitutional convention will need to adopt rules of procedure. But many of the procedural questions arising at a convention of states will be unique. After all the ethical, procedural, and governance principles documents are adopted, delegates will still not be fully ready to take up their substantive agenda—they will still have to debate HOW to craft the agenda itself—thereby deciding which amendments to take up. Here are four considerations for getting started with this task:

1. How will the convention decide the amendments it will consider? Should amendment ideas require only a simple majority to send them to a committee for consideration and debate? Can committees develop their own proposals? For purposes of preliminary discussion in committee, should a lower threshold than a majority be required to at least talk about an idea for constitutional revision—say one-third or forty percent? Should a simple or super-majority be required for a committee to send recommendations to the full convention, or on to the states? In what other ways should delegates sort, group, and categorize amendment ideas? Convention rules should encourage respectful debate of all issues, from both minority and majority factions, because sometimes minority views evolve into majority positions through discussion and revisions, and because they can often be folded into other proposals, in whole or in part, through the deliberative process. If super majorities are required at all, they should be required only in full sessions of all convention delegates, and then only when final approval is contemplated. These and other

questions will have to be resolved in advance and included in adopted 'Special Rules of Order.'

2. <u>Should final voting by the convention (to approve or disapprove amendment proposals and send them to the states) give each state the same voting strength or should more populous states have greater voting power?</u> The 1787 convention voted by state and each state had one vote. Proportional voting based on population would be more democratic, but then the 9 or 10 largest states could control the outcome. Voting by state would give a better indication of whether amendments had a likelihood of success in the state-by-state ratification process, but the 26 smallest states, in the aggregate, comprise only 17 to 18 percent of the nation's population. Is there a way to do both? Yes. When amendments are ready for final approval by the full convention, there could be a process of "first and second readings" required. At the "first reading," a majority vote of all delegates could be required to affirm a proposed constitutional amendment. If this is achieved, there could be a "second reading" wherein delegates vote by state with approval required from a majority of states (26) for an amendment proposal to secure final approval and go to states. Implementation of this "first and second reading" approach will require rural and urban regions to compromise. Adoption of this, or some other method, of final amendment approval would also have to be resolved by the convention, in advance, with 'Special Rules of Order.'

3. <u>Should convention sessions be open to the public or should some be closed?</u> The 1787 convention was conducted entirely in secret. Delegates deliberately chose not to release their notes to the public for many years—lest they

unduly influence governance decisions in the early years immediately after the Constitution's approval. Delegates mostly turned over their notes to George Washington at the end of the convention and they were stored in the National Archives. It was 20 years before some of them were published. The notes of James Madison were not published until 1840, four years after his death in accordance with his wishes.[23]

The public and the media will not tolerate this level of secrecy in the 21st Century. If delegates tried to do so today, staff members and other delegates would leak information to the media, motivated by political advocacy, partisanship, a desire to embarrass political enemies, or just to obtain notoriety. A new convention's best interests will be served by allowing open coverage of full convention deliberations. This will help keep delegates accountable to the public. The public will want delegates to behave with civility and wisdom—so it is better to practice transparency anyway during the sessions when all delegates are assembled. Greater public deliberation will also build appreciation for the complexities of governance among the general population, and help the public make up its own collective mind about the merit of various amendments under consideration. But at some level, perhaps at the committee or sub-committee level, delegates will need freedom to discuss new ideas and their consequences without having to fear being accosted at restaurants or demonized on social media platforms for ideas and remarks that are still nascent, and little more than delegates' initial conceptual thoughts.

---

[23] John P. Kaminski, Secrecy and the Constitutional Convention, Center for the Study of the American Constitution, University of Wisconsin—Madison, 2005.

4. <u>Assuming the convention produces more than one unrelated amendment recommendation, should each amendment stand on its own or be "packaged" with others?</u> Unnatural pairings of unrelated items could lead to cries of proposals "held hostage;" and an omnibus mix of unrelated topics all in the same amendment proposal would likely doom the proposal when it reaches the states. States should be able to "pick and choose" the amendment ideas they wish to approve, and those they wish to reject (as they did with Bill of Rights provisions between 1789 and 1791).[24] The only exception to this rule would be circumstances where an amendment in one section of the Constitution requires a companion amendment in another section for it to be operationally functional and internally consistent. In such cases alone, two or more connected and related amendments could be submitted as a "package" amendment. Rules prohibiting "unnatural pairings" would also have to be formally adopted in advance as part of the convention's 'Special Rules of Order.'

Without agreement concerning process, procedure, and common points of reference, and lacking membership homogeneity or a pre-meeting consensus about the tasks of the body, contentious conventions often devolve into chaos. When people of dissimilar interests and objectives are joined for the purpose of joint policymaking and debate, the group's proceedings should be facilitated in accordance with agreed-upon rules, embraced and endorsed by most voting members

---

[24] The amendments Congress submitted to the states that later became The Bill of Rights were actually comprised of 12 sections—only 10 of these provisions were adopted by three-fourths of the states in the 18th Century. The states decided which would pass.

of the convention. These 'rules of engagement,' adopted as 'Special Rules of Order,' should be enacted in advance, subject to amendment only by a three-fifths or two-thirds majority vote. More than civility and good behavior are on the line. Even if chaos is avoided, without agreement as to process there will be confusion, contentious posturing, dysfunction, and a lack of confidence in the convention, both internally and externally. Special Rules of Order (or the same thing by another title) could prevent chaos and give outside observers hope the convention can achieve its purposes. Every large legislative body uses detailed procedural rules for these reasons.

To advance popular ideas and avoid deadlock at the convention, coalitions may form to allow proposals to get out of committee and onto the floor of the full convention. Some ideas acceptable in committee may not enjoy widespread support among all other delegates, and vice-versa. But it should be simpler to get a proposal out of committee than it is to achieve final adoption of amendments for purposes of sending them to the 50 states—otherwise nothing might emerge from committees. For example, a group of states could favor a 'balanced budget amendment' but oppose tax reform amendments, while another group favors the reverse. The two groups could work together to get both proposals out of committee and to the convention floor. Once they are presented to the full convention, delegates will have to decide what they truly support and give both proposals a full airing. The full convention should also be allowed to eject from its committees any bottled-up proposals. After all, the states will serve as final arbiters of whether an amendment should be included in the Constitution.

Brevity is a great virtue in Constitution writing (though it is rarely seen in modern legislatures). Simple and easily understood language, rather than complex legalese, should be the norm for all amendments. Proposals should stand alone, with few sub-clauses and a minimal number of subcomponents. Some sections of the existing Constitution deal with one narrow topic (e.g., provisions listing what Congress cannot do, and what States may not do). Other sections of the U.S. Constitution deal with multiple foundational principles all in the same paragraph. The First Amendment exemplifies the virtues of brevity; it addresses freedom of speech, religion, press, assembly, and the right to talk back to the government for redress of grievances—all in the same 45-word paragraph.

E. How should proposed amendments be presented to States and citizens after their approval by the convention?

In 1787, 12 of the original 13 states appointed 70 delegates to the Constitutional Convention held in Philadelphia. Of these, only 55 delegates (78%) attended all or a portion of the proceedings. Rhode Island sent no delegates. The final document was signed in September by 39 delegates (55%). Some participating delegates did not sign because they had left town before the end of the process, but a few others declined to sign because they could not support the proposed document. The Constitution was then transmitted to the Congress of Confederation, who in turn voted to send it to the States for ratification. Had the Congress of Confederation believed that the First Constitutional Convention exceeded its mandate, they could have refused to send the document to the states. A Second Constitutional Convention's work product will not be screened or subject to approval by Congress. Today, Congress only decides the mode of ratification to be used at the state level. Absent legal intervention alleging violations of Article Five provisions, delegates to a Second Constitutional Convention will not know, when they adjourn, which amendments will achieve approval from 38 states (or 39 states if Puerto Rico or some other territory becomes the 51st state prior to a convention of states).

The work of convention delegates should not end when their recommended amendments are sent to the 50 states and the convention is adjourned. For their efforts to succeed, delegates should all become advocates and champions in their respective states, following the convention's adjournment, and should encourage speedy consideration of the convention's proposals. Delegates should return home, meet with citizens, and give testimony in state legislative or state convention hearings where amendment proposals will be debated. A few delegates may decide to write books and articles (perhaps called *The Federalist Papers 2.0*) to help achieve passage and approval of proposed constitutional revisions. If there is near-consensus coming out of the convention of states, it will deliver a strong message that recommended revisions—while not perfect—are reasonable updates for making the nation stronger and less polarized. If they are also the product of thoughtful compromise, reflecting solid principles of good governance, then they will have the greatest likelihood of becoming part of the Constitution.

The existing Article Five script for a convention of states admittedly includes few details; apparently the Framers did not consider them necessary. This worries the opponents of a modern Article Five convention; but it should not. A Second Constitutional Convention can be managed. The First Constitutional Convention worked through multiple thorny differences satisfactorily. For a Second Constitutional Convention to be successful, however, much more planning will be required since there will be more partisan demons to corral the second time around. Achieving consensus wherever possible must be the goal of delegates. Chaos, disunity, and decisions made with razor-thin majorities will not produce anything that 38 states will want to ratify.

Chapter Four

25+ Constitutional Amendment Proposals

Constitutional amendments favored by narrow constituencies, catering only to special interests, and unable to command broad popular support should not be brought to the convention. The bar for ratification is too high for frivolous, dangerous, or deeply divisive amendments to succeed.

Amendment proposals will need more than popular support to advance. They need to be readily understood by the population. Clarity and brevity of language should be the norm. The U.S. Constitution is not only the world's oldest functioning national constitution; it is also the shortest, in part because it is comparatively simple. The Constitution is blessed with checks and balances to rein-in tyranny, control factions, balance power, and provide representation for a scattered and diverse population; but it was also crafted without impenetrable legalese and complex carve-outs to protect special interests. The Constitution's authors believed its key tenets and principles should be expressed in common words and phrases—not tedious, ponderous, and arcane language—for them to enjoy popular support. Common language communicates the basic mechanics of governance to citizens; it also affords flexibility to future courts as they seek to interpret the Constitution's intent and apply its provisions to new circumstances, allowing amendments to stand the test of time.

This chapter offers simple draft language for 25 constitutional amendments that can be evaluated by delegates attending a convention of states in keeping with the tone and structure of the original Constitution. The amendment proposals below denote new language with **_bold italics_** and identify language proposed for deletion using text ~~cross-outs~~. The proposals are embedded within current constitutional text where appropriate. They fall into five groups.

1. Amendments to achieve greater fiscal restraint by the Federal government.

2. Amendments intended to rein-in Federal government overreach, re-assert the prerogatives of states, guard against tyranny and authoritarianism by the national government, and reset the Federal/State balance.

3. Amendments to the judiciary that, along with other changes, improve the judicial branch, focus on justice and the rule-of-law, emphasize original doctrines of separated powers, and assert supremacy of the Constitution and Supreme Court in constitutional and legislative matters clearly under Federal control.

4. Amendments strengthening democracy by enhancing equality of voice (e.g., in the election of the president leading to revisions in the Electoral College, management of elections, elimination of partisan Gerrymandering, and clarifying the rights associated with citizenship).

5. Amendments to basic rights concerning free speech, censorship, excessive punishments, access to firearms, and codifying ethical standards for elected and appointed government leaders.

Amendment ideas offered in this chapter are grouped using the five categories above, but are not in any order of priority or importance. A central tenet of this book is that basic concepts and principles embodied in the current Constitution are sound and should be retained; but the modernizing of multiple sections at the same time can only be accomplished by calling a convention of states to reassert the Constitution's goals of limited government, re-balance governmental powers, and achieve a less polarized and fractured society. Entire books could be written about some of the amendment ideas offered here—rather than just a few paragraphs. But this book is intended to serve as a simple manual for solving problems and navigating the logistics of a convention of states. It is not a comprehensive and academic analysis of legal theory, or an exhaustive probing of the genesis of every possible amendment proposal.[25] The finer legal details of competing amendment ideas are left to convention delegates to resolve. This is a "how and why to do it" manual.

Each of the 25 proposed amendments is prefaced with a brief background and narrative rationale. A modern convention of states will likely consider some of these ideas. This compilation includes amendment proposals suggested by both the political Left and Right. Even a quick reading of these proposals demonstrates that Orwellian outcomes are unlikely. They are merely a reasonable starting point for deliberations.

---

[25] There are numerous contemporary books offering thoughtful suggestions for constitutional amendment. I have borrowed from them selectively and recommend them all. Some are overtly partisan; most are lengthier and academic in style, and include copious references and annotations, analysis of court cases, and extended legal arguments. They include John Paul Stevens' *Six Amendments* (Little, Brown & Co., New York, 2014); Larry Sabato's *A More Perfect Constitution* (Bloomsbury, New York, 2008); Richard Labunski's *The Second Constitutional Convention: How American People Can Take Back Their Government* (Marley & Beck Press, 2000), and others.

Following the 25 amendment proposals is a brief discussion of additional governance policy topics, which, it is argued, should **not** be taken up during a modern convention of states because these governance issues do not require constitutional amendments to advance, do not warrant constitutional revision, or overlap with other amendment proposals. Too often constitutional amendments are recommended, or a sensitive topic is kicked to the courts, when all that is actually needed is for Congress to step up, do their job, and adopt legislation resolving contentious matters—such as immigration reform. Nonetheless, any book about proposed constitutional amendments is incomplete without mentioning these topics.

The U.S. Constitution has endured for over 230 years, in part, because it articulates broad governance principles and processes, leaving smaller details to the executive, legislative, and judicial branches of government, and to the states. With key exceptions, the signers of the 1787 Constitution were willing to trust Congress and the States with operational details of governance, so long as they stayed within the Constitution's parameters and basic architecture. On balance, their trust was not misplaced. They believed attempts to abuse political power would be reined-in by the Constitution's checks and balances. But in the last fifty years, Congress has transferred so much of its power to regulatory bureaucrats in the Executive Branch, to Courts by default, and to autonomous commissions, that the Legislative Branch is now comparatively ineffective in acting as first intended. Original constitutional safeguards (interwoven into the fabric of the Constitution to contend with democracy's greatest threat: divisive, partisan factions) no longer work properly. If it is the judgment of 34 states that divisive partisan factions have wrecked the Constitution's checks and balances and taken the nation off the rails, then amendments are now required.

Twenty-Five Proposals for Constitutional Revision

GROUP ONE Amendments to achieve greater fiscal restraint by the Federal government

Since 2014, more than a dozen states have adopted resolutions calling for a convention of states for purposes of "imposing fiscal restraints on the Federal government;" and resolutions have been introduced in legislatures of at least a dozen more states using the same language. Some of these state resolutions specifically mention a balanced budget amendment; but no state has proposed any other specific constitutional language clarifying exactly HOW to impose and implement better fiscal restraints.

[1] A balanced budget amendment.

The national debt has reached historic heights. Congress' willingness to consistently spend more than it has in its Treasury is the result of poor management and insufficient fiscal constraints. But it is also about power. The more money the Federal government doles out; the more power it accumulates. Government largesse has purchased much expansion in Federal power. Foreign aid buys power overseas. More domestic spending comes with legal strings requiring recipients to grant more power to the central government than the Constitution envisioned or allows.

Since 1944, the U.S. Dollar has served as the world's reserve currency, making the temptation to overspend hard to resist, thereby increasing Federal power through spending. In times of uncertainty, investors across the world seek the relative security of the U.S. dollar, strengthening the Dollar at home. If the Dollar loses this status, just as British Pound Sterling did at the end of World War II, then the value of the Dollar will collapse, and the country will rely on other nations to a far greater extent to plug its deficits—likely with disastrous economic results. Before this occurs, Congress must learn greater fiscal restraint. More fiscal constraint, in turn, will bring more devolution of government control back to the states.

For decades, politicians have called for a balanced budget amendment to the Constitution, prohibiting deficit spending except in the event of war or other equally disruptive and perilous national emergency. As the nation's cumulative debt surpasses $31 trillion, a balanced budget amendment is even more important today than when the idea first gained widespread support in the 20th Century. It could look like this:

AN AMENDMENT BY INSERTION INTO ARTICLE ONE, SECTION 7:

"Total outlays for any fiscal year shall not exceed total receipts for the same fiscal year, inclusive of borrowing and debt service, unless three-fourths of the duly chosen and sworn Members of each House of Congress shall provide by law for a specific excess of outlays over receipts by roll call vote, except that a simple majority will be required for expenses exceeding revenues during periods when a Congressional declaration of war against a foreign entity remains in effect."

An unintended, but desirous, consequence of this revision is that the power of the Executive Branch to make war without the express approval of Congress may be reduced, because without a Congressional declaration of war, the president would have to prosecute undeclared military actions within normal balanced budget constraints.

[2] Limitations on Federal taxing powers.

The Federal government derives much of its extra-constitutional power from its authority to levy and collect taxes and issue limitless debt. If it was harder for the Federal government to create and enact new taxes and spend money it does not have, then it would be harder for them to accumulate more power. Article One, Section 8 provides for Congress to "collect taxes, duties, imposts, and excises." The 16th Amendment also authorizes the levying of income taxes because the term "taxes" (prior to 1913) in the Constitution was not believed to include progressive income taxes. Article One, Section 8 gives authority to issue debt, but does not limit debt accumulation to prevent a runaway build-up of national debt.

Members of Congress often express their desire to create ever more taxes. Existing constitutional limits on Federal taxing authority act only as limited legal impediments. Proposals for national sales taxes and national value-added taxes have been floated, but languish, lacking explicit constitutional authority. Greater clarity is required regarding where the Federal government can, and cannot, impose new taxes.

Although every state in the country must conform to requirements that they demonstrate to bond buyers their ability to repay debt with legally binding amortization schedules and proof they have sufficient revenues to service their debt (just like anyone else seeking a bank loan) the Federal government operates under no such constraints. In addition to a balanced budget amendment, another mechanism to impose fiscal restraint and discipline on the Federal government would be to constrain its ability to tax and incur limitless debt, with exceptions for wartime and related emergencies, but still permit the Federal government to create new taxes when there is broad bipartisan support for them. These revisions require another amendment of Article One, Section 8:

AN AMENDMENT THROUGH REVISION AND REPLACEMENT OF THE FIRST CLAUSE OF ARTICLE ONE, SECTION 8:

"The Congress shall have Power to *raise revenue only through the following means: laying and collecting taxes on the earnings of persons and businesses, levying of duties and tariffs on goods entering the United States, levying and collecting fees on energy and other natural resources of the United States, and fees on the use of federal land and property. All other imposts and excises by any other name shall be enacted and dedicated only for specific public purposes, enacted only after having obtained approval by a two-thirds vote of both houses of Congress and approval of the president.* ~~The Congress shall have Power to lay and collect Taxes, Duties, Imposts and Excises, to pay the Debts and provide for the common Defense and general Welfare of the United States but~~ All Duties, Imposts, and Excises shall be uniform throughout the United States."

AND

AN AMENDMENT THROUGH REVISION OF CLAUSE #2 OF ARTICLE ONE, SECTION 8:

"The Congress may borrow Money on the credit of the United States, *but only for terms not to exceed fifty years, and only by dedicating specific revenues toward the repayment of all debts until they are retired using a repayment schedule approved by Congress.*"

The Constitution clearly gives power to levy taxes to the Congress, because it is the Federal branch closest to the people. For this reason, some argue that Federal courts should not have the power to render decisions indirectly requiring the levying of new taxes. If this limitation on the power of Federal courts to indirectly tax the people is desired, then judiciary powers in Article Three also require amendment.

AN AMENDMENT BY INSERTION INTO ARTICLE THREE:

"*Cases involving Federal law and this Constitution shall be filed in the Federal court jurisdiction in which the case or cause of action originates, and each inferior court's decision will have scope and affect only in each inferior court's circuit or district until the Supreme Court, by whatever means, shall extend such decision's scope and affect to the entire country, except that Federal court decisions shall not extend to, or be construed to require, the levy and collection of new taxes.*"

This proposed revision would also correct a modern aberration of the Federal judiciary—the practice of so-called "judge shopping," because it would limit the effect of any Federal court decision to the district from which it emerges, until it is affirmed or extended by the Supreme Court.

[3] Line-Item Veto for the President.

A line-item veto was first proposed by Congress in 1876. A Line-Item Veto Act was enacted by Act of Congress and signed by President Clinton in 1996 to control spending, but it was invalidated by the Supreme Court two years later as an unconstitutional intrusion into the powers of Congress. Forty-three governors have some form of line-item veto authority. Most arguments in favor of giving the president line-item veto authority focus on the fiscal discipline such a measure will encourage. But the arguments for and against presidential line-item veto are also about power, and the carefully crafted balance of power that should exist between the executive and legislative branches of the Federal government. Maintaining this delicate balance, as envisioned by the Framers, argues that if a line-item veto is desired, it should be narrowly crafted by amending Article Two, and focus only on fiscal matters, the mitigation of largess, and constraining pork barrel spending.

AN AMENDMENT BY INSERTION OF AN ADDITIONAL CLAUSE INTO THE EXISTING LANGUAGE OF ARTICLE TWO, SECTION 2:
"The President may approve or veto Acts of Congress in whole or in part as provided herein. The President may approve or reject an Act of Congress in its entirety as provided herein; or he may delete specific expenditure sections; but the President shall not re-write or alter the language of any Act of

Congress except by deletion, and then only by deleting
expenditure provisions, and projects and programs
directly connected thereto."

GROUP TWO: Amendments intended to rein-in
Federal government over-reach, re-assert states'
prerogatives, guard against authoritarianism and
tyranny by the national government, and reset the
Federal/State balance.

Since 2014, more than ten states have adopted resolutions
calling for a convention of states for "limiting the power and/
or jurisdiction of the Federal government;" and resolutions have
been introduced in legislatures of at least six more states using
the same language. In the aggregate, these resolutions reflect
concern by States that their ability to govern has been usurped
by the Federal government and that increased accumulation of
government control in Washington has led to widespread abuses
of power. With the exception of term-limits, however, none
of these state resolutions propose specific ideas or amendment
language detailing HOW to rein-in Federal power, re-establish
a healthier balance between the Federal branches, and improve
Federal-State relations. What follows are nine amendment ideas
for creating better governance balance.

[4] Limit the reach of the "general welfare" and the "necessary and proper" clauses.

The first paragraph of Article One, Section 8 of the
Constitution says: "The Congress shall have Power to lay and
collect Taxes, Duties, Imposts and Excises, to pay the Debts and

provide for the common Defense and *general Welfare* of the United States but all duties, imposts, and excises shall be uniform throughout the United States." In the last paragraph of the same section, the Constitution says Congress shall have the power "To make all Laws which shall be *necessary and proper* for carrying into Execution the foregoing Powers . . ."

Debate over the meaning of the "general welfare" and "necessary and proper" clauses is as old as the Constitution itself. Madisonians and Jeffersonians argued that enumerated (i.e., the specific list of) powers in the Constitution should be read narrowly. Federalists like Adams and Hamilton believed Article One, Section 8 should be interpreted broadly. None of the Founding Fathers was clairvoyant and they could not anticipate the best role for the Federal government hundreds of years into the future. On some occasions, the best interests of the nation have been served by narrow constitutional decisions and interpretations; at other times, they were best served by liberally construed decisions.

The Federal Courts have never definitively articulated the natural limits of either clause; they can be permanently clarified only by constitutional amendment. Alexander Hamilton in Federalist #33 explained that any government must possess the means and methods to effectively govern; this requires "necessary and proper" powers. Hamilton wrote that "a power to lay and collect taxes must be a power to pass all laws necessary and proper for the execution of that power." In short, Hamilton believed the Constitution also authorizes the means and methods for effectuating specifically enumerated powers. It should not, however, include the means and methods for enacting powers not mentioned in the Constitution. Hamilton (still in Federalist #33) was quick to emphasize the limited and ministerial nature of "necessary and proper" in this context: "If there be anything [i.e., new laws] exceptionable, it must be sought for in the specific powers upon which this general declaration is predicated." In other words, anything beyond the ministerial means and methods required to carry out a constitutionally enumerated power must find authorization in the specific language of Article One, Section 8.

Neither of these vague clauses was meant to provide legal cover for unlimited creation of wholly new power prerogatives, such as the enactment of Green Energy laws without an Act of Congress, or the extortionist use of the "power of the purse" to enforce new powers and initiatives beyond the pale of the Constitution and lying outside the Constitution's enumerated powers. Correcting this practice requires amending Article One, Section 8. The amendment proposed below overlaps with other recommended changes to rein-in Federal taxing and debt issuance, such as proposal #2 above, so this recommendation deals exclusively with restricting use of the "general welfare" clause.

AN AMENDMENT, BY REVISION, OF THE FIRST PARAGRAPH OF ARTICLE ONE, SECTION 8:

"The Congress shall have the Power to lay and collect Taxes, Duties, Imposts and Excises, to pay the Debts and provide for the common Defense ~~and general Welfare~~ of the United States ~~but~~ *and fund governmental functions and powers specifically delineated in this Article. Neither Congress nor the President may obtain or compel powers or functions not specifically delineated in this Article.* All Duties, Imposts and Excises shall be uniform throughout the United States. Congress shall also . . ."

108

Requiring public schools to enact transgender policies as a condition of receiving school lunch funding is not an exercise of enumerated powers and therefore compelling it as a condition of obtaining funding for an unrelated education program would be barred by the language above. Of course, providing for public education itself is not an enumerated power of the Federal government.

[5] Limit the 'Commerce Clause'.

The 'commerce clause' is another enumerated power listed in Article One, Section 8. Debate over the scope and reach of the "commerce clause" began as early as the campaign for initial constitutional ratification. This provision was meant to prohibit states from regulating foreign commerce independently (as some states had done prior to the Revolution), and to make sure "interstate commerce" did not degrade into warring rivalries between states, where states charged tolls for the privilege of transiting goods into and across other states. The Founding Fathers did not intend for the Federal government to be authorized to regulate and control nearly all parts of the nation's economy using the 'commerce clause,' although this is what has evolved in the 21st Century. This provision of the Constitution also acknowledged that some degree of autonomy should be allowed for States and Native American tribes, and that intra-state commerce should remain within the realm of States and tribes. Regulating inter-state commerce, while permitted by the 'commerce clause,' should not be synonymous with central control of the nation's entire economy. The language below moves this clause closer to its original intentions.

AN AMENDMENT BY REVISION TO THE
THIRD CLAUSE OF ARTICLE ONE, SECTION 8:
"To regulate Commerce with foreign Nations, and among the several States, and with the ~~Indian~~ *Native American* Tribes; *but intra-state commerce and intra-tribal commerce shall be regulated by each state and tribe respectively.*"

[6] Bar Foreign Treaties from altering domestic laws without corresponding authorization by Congress.

Article Two, Section 2 of the Constitution gives the president authority to "make treaties" with foreign governments if two-thirds of the Senate concurs. But this authority does not grant the Executive Branch of government the power to extend treaty terms to state and local governments without an Act of Congress, in contravention of the 10th Amendment. Beginning in the late 20th Century, the Federal government started to use its power to make treaties and alliances with foreign governments in ways that extended the provisions of treaty documents to sub-national governments via Federal regulations enacted by bureaucrats without an Act of Congress. If the Federal government made a treaty with a foreign power, then local and state laws conflicting with treaty provisions could be voided or superseded by Federal regulators. By subtly implementing such provisions via the burgeoning regulatory bureaucracy of the Executive Branch, the balance between the executive and legislative branches is disrupted, and the balance between Federal and State levels of government is also misaligned.

Bureaucrats writing administrative regulations sometimes act without authorization from Congress, thereby extending their powers. In short, they operate beyond Congress' mandates, and Congress should reclaim its constitutional role. Just because the U.S. Senate makes treaties with foreign governments regarding energy regulations or the environment, it does not mean these provisions should be automatically extended domestically. The Federal government should not be able to outsource its domestic public health policy to the World Health Organization (WHO) without an Act of Congress, and Senate action on a foreign treaty should not upend internal American federalism. Correcting this modern practice requires a short amendment attached to Article One, Section 10:

AN AMENDMENT BY INSERTION OF NEW LANGUAGE: "No state shall be subject to provisions of a foreign treaty, foreign law, or foreign agreement except by Act of Congress, approved by the president."

[7] Limit the use and reach of Executive Orders issued by the President and of other regulations issued by unelected bureaucrats.

Historically, executive orders pertained only to the Executive Branch of government. In other words, as the head of the Executive Branch, the president can, by edict and fiat, establish rules and regulations pertaining only to the Executive Branch of the Federal government, so long as they do not conflict with an Act of Congress or are contrary to court rulings. For example, the president can, by executive order, require all Federal employees to be vaccinated against COVID-19; but his executive order powers do not extend to the legislative or judicial branches, and they have no impact on state governments. In recent years, presidents have sought to rule the country by edict, decree, and fiat (by way of executive orders). This gives the Executive Branch potentially dictatorial powers and contributes directly to constitutional imbalance. The problem is exacerbated by the growth in regulatory agencies. Fixing this imbalance requires an amendment to Article Two:

> *AN AMENDMENT BY INSERTION OF NEW LANGUAGE INTO ARTICLE TWO, SECTION 2: "The president shall have the power to issue executive orders only to clarify and enact policies of the executive branch of government; no such orders shall be enacted that are in conflict with any Act of Congress, are not funded by Congress (if funding be required), are in conflict with any ruling of a Federal court, infringe on the power of the various states as provided herein, or are contrary to any provision of this Constitution."*

[8] Congressional Term Limits.

The Founding Fathers envisioned a "citizen legislature" comprised of civic leaders who would take time from their lives to serve their country as a Member of Congress. They likely did not envision the evolution of career politicians who became entrenched in their posts, acquired significant personal wealth during their terms of government service, and amassed considerable power and influence such that regular elections rarely dislodged them—even when they were found to be corrupt or had lost touch with constituencies they were elected to represent. This is the argument in favor of term-limits for Members of Congress.

The argument against term-limits is that States can lose deep institutional knowledge (and legislative effectiveness for the state or district represented) when a Member of Congress is turfed-out after being term-limited. And while incumbency is a powerful edge in elections, it can be overcome at the ballot box.

Proposals for Congressional term limits could establish a lifetime limit (as the 22nd Amendment imposes on the Presidency), or simply require a break in continuous service, as many lower-level boards and commissions provide in order to turn-over membership. Instead of lifetime limits, an amendment could allow persons sufficiently popular to return to government service after a period of time. Amending the Constitution to impose legislative term limits requires two separate amendments to Article One, the first concerning Representatives and the second concerning Senators.

AN AMENDMENT BY INSERTION INTO ARTICLE ONE, SECTION 2:

"No Representative shall be elected to more than six consecutive and continuous two-year terms, excluding partial terms authorized by special elections or gubernatorial appointment."

AND

AN AMENDMENT BY INSERTION INTO ARTICLE ONE, SECTION 3:

"No Senator shall be elected to more than two consecutive and continuous six-year terms, excluding partial terms authorized by special elections or gubernatorial appointment."

[9] Restrict the use of Federal pardons.

The Constitution's language governing pardons and reprieves is discussed by Hamilton in *Federalist 69* and *Federalist 74*. It allows the president to exercise mercy and to protect members of his government from a capricious legislature or court, making it another check and balance. It seems clear to most legal scholars that the president's power to issue pardons does not extend to impeached persons, and for this reason President Trump could not have pardoned himself had he been found guilty of high crimes or misdemeanors by the Senate. Pardons should not be available to the president issuing the pardon, and they should not be available where no court has adjudicated a decision, unless the recipient of the pardon has been first incarcerated or detained. It is an abuse of the pardoning power to allow it to be used to grant judicial immunity in advance for all future prosecutions and where the subject has not been incarcerated. The appropriate revision of Article Two, Section 2 might look like this:

AN AMENDMENT OF ARTICLE TWO, SECTION 2 BY REVISION:

". . . and he shall have Power to grant Reprieves and Pardons for Offenses against the United States, except in Cases of Impeachment. *The president may not pardon himself of any charge, and the president shall issue no pardons or reprieves from potential or expected charges that have not been adjudicated by courts, and/or where the subject of the pardon has not been detained or imprisoned.*"

[10] States' Rights and the Tenth Amendment.

The Tenth Amendment to the Constitution (part of the original Bill of Rights) is sometimes referred to (when referred to at all) as the "forgotten amendment." It reads simply: "The powers not delegated to the United States by the Constitution, nor prohibited by it to the states, are reserved to the states respectively, or to the people."

The Tenth Amendment was not "forgotten;" it was deliberately contravened, over-ruled and trodden upon in the interests of expediency (see Chapter Two) to increase the power of the Federal government. The courts' deference to the 'general welfare' and 'necessary and proper' clauses of the Constitution, as well as an expansive interpretation of the 'commerce clause', have caused the Tenth Amendment to be diluted and marginalized by regulatory overreach, executive orders, and the cumulative effects of unchallenged assertions of power by Congress and the president over more than two centuries. Courts and other branches of the Federal government have not sufficiently restricted the use of the 'general welfare' and 'necessary and proper' clauses to ministerial purposes only, thereby permitting the Federal government to adopt unenumerated powers. If the framers of the 1787 Constitution could have foreseen the extent to which the Tenth Amendment would lie gutted after two centuries, they likely would have composed this Amendment differently. In hindsight, perhaps the First Congress should have phrased the Tenth Amendment like this:

AN AMENDMENT OF THE 10TH AMENDMENT:

"The powers not delegated to the United States by the Constitution, nor prohibited by it to the

States, are reserved to the States respectively, or to the people. *Interference in the affairs of States by the government of the United States shall be limited to matters of due process and to the extension of powers directly and explicitly enumerated in, and given to, the Congress, the President, and the Courts by this Constitution."*

[11] Other Measures to Slow the growth of the Regulatory State.

Whether it is vaccination mandates, program funding conditions compelling unrelated actions by state and local governments, or the creation of Federal laws not explicitly authorized by Congress or by the Constitution's enumeration of Federal power, the U.S. Government uses administrative regulations to shift governing power from the States to Washington D.C., and from Congress to the Executive Branch. This is a systemic governance problem and not a product of partisanship. The Supreme Court's *West Virginia v. EPA* (2022) has drawn a new line-in-the-sand for bureaucrats acting as shadow Congressmen, but more correction is needed.

Legislation approved by the Legislative Branch is usually implemented by the Executive Branch. But the policy objectives of the legislative and executive branches are not always synchronized, and on occasion unelected administrators advance their own agendas through the regulatory process (what critics call the "deep state"). A proposal for correcting this shortcoming would be to require all Federal regulations to be approved by Congress; but this is not practical in the modern world. The national government's rule-making process is not fundamentally broken; it simply lacks proper accountability to constitutional checks and balances.

> *AN AMENDMENT BY INSERTION OF A NEW*
> *SECTION 11, INTO ARTICLE ONE:*
> *"Any combination of fifty or more senators and representatives may object to any regulatory rulings or decisions of the executive branch. If these senators and representatives file objections in writing with the clerk of the House of Representatives and the clerk of the Senate, then the regulatory ruling that is the subject of the objection shall be suspended and not enacted until it shall be approved by majority vote of both houses; but no approval by the president shall be required in such instances."*

Excluding the president from this new process is necessary because it is possible that objectionable regulations may emanate from an Act of Congress previously vetoed by the president and subsequently overridden. In such instances, the president should not be placed in a position to completely confound reasonable enforcement by again vetoing approval of regulatory decisions previously enacted into law. The point of this amendment is to make sure duly enacted Congressional intent is not dissipated or contravened by bureaucrats in the Executive Branch.

[12] Eliminate recess appointments.

The 'recess appointments' provision of the Constitution was written when Members of Congress were part-time, when travel to the nation's capital was difficult, when technology allowing remote meetings did not exist, and when concerns over continuity of government were more pronounced. Times have changed. Today, recess appointments are sometimes used to insert overtly partisan appointees into Cabinet-level jobs who may not be able to obtain Senate confirmation. End runs around the Senate's duty to provide advice and consent regarding presidential appointments are abuses of executive power. Rather than inserting specific language into the Constitution via amendment, the best fix for this problem is to simply repeal and remove subparagraph 3 of Section 2, in Article Two of the existing Constitution:

> ***AN AMENDMENT MADE BY DELETING THE FOLLOWING LANGUAGE:*** ~~"The President shall have the Power to fill up all Vacancies that may happen during the Recess of the Senate, by granting Commissions which shall expire at the End of their next Session."~~

<u>GROUP THREE</u>: Amendments to the judiciary that, along with other legal system changes, improve the judicial branch, emphasize the original doctrine of separated powers, and assert the supremacy of the Constitution and the Supreme Court in constitutional questions, and in areas clearly under Federal control.

The perceived impartiality of the nation's judiciary has suffered because it has been called upon to make partisan policy decisions, rather than render verdicts about what is, and is not, constitutional, just and legal. If the Supreme Court is now expected to act as a legislature—then this is more evidence of the national government's dysfunction. The Supreme Court should indeed be supreme, the Constitution should be paramount, and Federal Courts should primarily be instruments of justice, and not a tool for indirectly enacting policies to redistribute wealth and legislate on topics that could never get through Congress.

[13] Fix the number of Supreme Court Justices and Provide for alternative tenure.

Recent proposals to "pack" the Supreme Court reflect the degree to which the Supreme Court's decisions have been politicized due to Congress' inability to pass legislation on controversial topics. When Congress cannot muster the votes to resolve controversial policies on matters like abortion, immigration, marriage rights, gun ownership, religious liberty, and voting rights, they abdicate their responsibilities and indirectly send these policy matters to the Supreme Court. Then, when the Supreme Court does not deliver the policy outcomes certain partisan political factions desire, the membership of the Court, and the manner of appointing new justices, is skewed by partisan loyalties rather than an objective assessment of legal fitness and scholarship.

The Founding Fathers gave Supreme Court members life tenure because they wanted to free them from political whims and shifting popular winds. Justices were supposed to make their rulings based on what the law and the Constitution said, or base them on the original intentions of Congress, and make decisions conforming to founding principles of governance, equality under the law, and due process for all. This is still valid doctrine.

Setting limits on the length of justices' terms as a guard against court opinions influenced by the old age infirmities of senior justices is reasonable; but terms should be sufficiently long to insulate judges from political shifting sands and the imperatives of the next election cycle. The Constitution does not set the number of Supreme Court justices at nine—this number was established by an Act of Congress in 1869, and it can be changed by another Act of Congress. To permanently codify the number of Supreme Court justices and provide for their automatic retirement after a suitably lengthy term would require an amendment of Article Three, Section 1:

> ### AN AMENDMENT THROUGH REVISION:
> "The judicial Power of the United States shall be vested in one supreme Court, **comprised of nine Justices,** and in such inferior Courts as the Congress may from time to time ordain and establish. The Judges, both of the supreme and inferior Courts, shall hold their Offices during good Behavior **continuously for a term not to exceed twenty-five years, after which they may be re-appointed for one additional ten-year term at the discretion of the President and without the need for Senate confirmation. Except in the event of death or resignation, Justices may serve beyond their terms, but only until their successors are confirmed and seated. Justices and Judges** shall, at stated Times, receive for their Services a Compensation which shall not be diminished during their Continuance in Office. **The provisions of this section shall not apply to Judges and Justices serving at the time of the adoption of this amendment.**"

If a president's selection to fill a Supreme Court vacancy with a new face at the end of a 25-year term is rejected or is contentious, then the president could allow the incumbent to remain for up to another decade without a Senate vote. This approach provides more options for continuity and political compromise.

[14] Make America Less Litigious.

America's tort liability system is the laughingstock of the world and contributes just as much to the loss of domestic jobs as do differential labor rates and stiff environmental regulations. America's excessively litigious and suit-happy legal system contributes directly to the high cost of health care, and the cost of most other goods and services. The frequent failure of tort reform in Congress is a constant drag on the American economy, on innovation, on liberty (since litigation can be used as a cudgel to silence free speech), on safety and security agencies, and on efforts to retain domestic jobs. Reform need not be complicated. A limit on liability claims commensurate with actual losses, and a limit on punitive damage awards equal to no more than twice the amount of actual damages would more effectively align the legal profession with justice, and less with wealth re-distribution. Gross negligence (as Congress may define), committed with demonstrated malice and a premeditated intent to deceive, should be treated more harshly; but many civil damage awards are paid because a court found that a defendant could, with 20/20 hindsight, have *maybe* done something slightly different that *might* have resulted in a different outcome. Damage awards should not be based on unlikely "what-if" scenarios. The nation's legal profession has created (through relentless advertising by personal injury lawyers) an expectation that life should be risk-free, and that someone, somewhere, should be found to pay huge sums to plaintiffs and their lawyers even if they careened off a road and struck a tree due to their own impairment or inattention. This is little more than poorly disguised wealth redistribution, facilitated by a lack of tort reform.

Legal and tort reform has been proposed for decades in Congress, but it does not advance because an overwhelming number of Representatives and Senators are lawyers, and because lobbyists for trial lawyers have succeeded in blocking legal reforms. Predatory lawsuits stifle creativity and slow the scale-up of new ideas. On the other hand, without some legal liability, businesses and other parties may not act ethically. Since Congress will not act to keep voracious attorneys at bay with meaningful reforms, the Constitution could include this simple provision:

AN AMENDMENT ADDING THE FOLLOWING TO ARTICLE THREE, SECTION 2: "In the Inferior Courts civil suits for money damages cannot exceed two times actual losses except where the defendant knowingly and willfully acted with wonton misconduct, malice and/or with premediated intent to harm."

[15] Once and for all, prohibit constitutional nullification by states.

The Bill of Rights is a list of powers specifically DENIED and off limits to the government. Americans in 1789 wanted assurance that individual liberties would remain paramount. However, at different times, states have gone further and asserted a right to exempt themselves from certain constitutional provisions and Federal Court decisions because states created the original Union. Beginning with the 'Virginia and Kentucky Resolutions' (1798) seeking to invalidate the Alien & Sedition Acts, continuing into efforts by anti-slavery activists to ignore the Fugitive Slave Act of 1850, and other States' Rights actions before the Civil War, some states have tried to exclude themselves from decisions of the Supreme Court and the Supremacy Clause of the Constitution. Some states still believe they should, with concurrence from enough other states, possess the right to overturn Supreme Court decisions. These are all forms of nullification.

The Supreme Court has never countenanced nullification; but the possibility of new attempts at nullification warrant inserting new language into the Constitution, thereby stopping them once and for all. Nullification should be quashed for three reasons:

1. If the Constitution is amended, as proposed in this book, to include several new provisions limiting the power and reach of the Federal government, such "limited government" revisions should never be interpreted to give cover or credence to new forms of nullification. Constitutionally limiting the power of the Federal government should not reduce the Supreme Court's power to decide what is, and is not, constitutional throughout the entire country;

2. Some states still believe they can pick and choose which parts of the Constitution to follow, and which provisions can be ignored; and

3. Those powers specifically and exclusively given to the Federal government should be paramount over actions by states in the interests of a secure Union. California cannot decide to ignore the Second Amendment within its borders, and Texas should not give legal cover for lawsuits against abortion providers just because the state lacked standing to restrict abortion prior to the repeal of

Roe v. Wade—both are nullification in disguise. States should not be permitted to find clever ways of opting out of, or undermining, decisions of the Supreme Court, or of avoiding explicit constitutional provisions. The United States is one country; Federal power (even if reduced in scope by constitutional amendments) should be uniformly applied. A constitutional amendment to end future nullification attempts could be worded as follows:

AN AMENDMENT BY INSERTION OF THE FOLLOWING LANGUAGE, AFTER PARAGRAPH #2 OF ARTICLE SIX:

"No action or decision made by a state government, or inferior court, or other governmental entity shall be valid that seeks to nullify or void a decision of the Supreme Court or any lawful and constitutional action of Congress."

GROUP FOUR: Amendments that strengthen democracy by enhancing equality of voice.

Political factions have long sought to place their hands on the scales of free and fair elections by tinkering with the processes and mechanics of voting. Elected legislators should fairly represent a region's population. Elections and elective office should be accessible to as many citizens, and be as democratic, as possible; but they should also be secure—or they will not be perceived as legitimate.

[16] The control of Federal Elections should remain with States except for violations of due process and equal protection, and as necessary to retain quorums in Congress.

The role of the Federal government in electing Members of Congress has been the topic of national debate in the last decade as state governments sought to increase access to the ballot box and do so in ways protecting election integrity and preventing voter fraud. Article One, Section 4 of the Constitution is at the heart of this debate because the language of this section is confusing to modern readers. This existing language can be read to uphold state sovereignty over elections, and also interpreted to uphold Congress' right to have the last word. This confusion needs to be resolved.

The 1787 constitutional convention debated whether states should control Federal elections or whether the national government should control Federal elections. Alexander Hamilton, writing in *Federalist 59, 60 and 61*, asserted that the convention's choice was neither—it is intended to be under the control of both. If it was controlled exclusively by the Federal government, Hamilton reasoned, the national government could manipulate elections to increase its power and thereby exercise tyranny over the states to favor certain classes of voter. If the states exercised exclusive control over Federal elections, then large states could conspire to manipulate the system to disrupt the balance between states, or states could cause dissolution of the Union by refusing to elect and send members to Congress, or foreign powers could align with domestic allies to undermine the Union via state control of Federal elections. In other words, this cumbersome and seemingly contradictory language in Article One, Section 4 was intended as another check and balance;

but it is imperfectly worded, it lacks modern context, and it is misunderstood in the 21st Century.

Hamilton acknowledged that Federal control of elections for Members of Congress could lead to actions by elites to devise election systems producing candidates and legislatures aligned with the interests of the "wealthy and well-born." Hamilton believed that this outcome would eventually be self-correcting, but he was wrong. In fact, the states were more often the ones guilty of manipulating election laws to limit who could and could not vote—not the Federal government.

The Constitution anticipates and acknowledges that elections need not be conducted in exactly the same manner in every state and locality. Hamilton saw a need for Federal influence in Congressional elections for comparatively few instances—such as having Congressional elections conducted on the same day every two years.[26] A concern that certain classes of citizens (i.e., power elites) might attempt to exclude other groups from suffrage by means of state tinkering with election laws was not resolved by the original Constitution, but it has been effectively resolved by subsequent amendments, Federal legislation and Supreme Court decisions. Where due process of law has been denied by state and local election authorities, the Federal government can assert and sustain its role in elections under the language of Article One, Section 4, and it has done so repeatedly since the enactment of civil rights legislation in the 1960s. In other words, if various state voter identification laws have been skewed to make it harder for certain groups of citizens to vote, the Federal Courts and Congress can and should intervene.

---

[26] Federalist No. 61. Although this was ultimately enacted by an Act of Congress, a common date for Congressional elections was not included in the Constitution. Hamilton argued in 1788 that it was still too soon to know what this date should be.

But state governments are given control over "the times, places and manner of holding elections for senators and representatives." These "shall be prescribed in each state by the legislature thereof; but the Congress may at any time by law make or alter such regulations." Hamilton and his fellow delegates wanted to make sure Congress could intervene if several states decided to undermine the Union by sending NO senators and representatives. He did not envision that the Federal government would one day attempt to use this section of the Constitution to mandate ballot harvesting, or that states could be prohibited from deciding to remove from voter rolls the names of persons who had not voted in several election cycles, perhaps because they had died or moved away.

Language pertaining to the choosing of senators, along with much of the rest of Article One, Section 4, is antiquated because senators are now elected directly. If states are empowered to determine the "manner" of holding elections, but Congress can "alter such regulations," then what is the point of this provision?

The Founding Fathers provided for state oversight of Congressional elections because they fundamentally believed the Federal government was created by the states, and that the states needed sufficient mechanisms for checking the power of the Federal government. But states were not always wise or fair stewards of this power, and sometimes states used their authority to deny voting rights to ethnic minorities, and later undermine the principle of one-man-one-vote. Several Supreme Court decisions, and the 14th, 15th, and 24th Amendments, have determined states cannot deny due process and equal access to voter suffrage in their exercise of the "manner" of electing Members of Congress. This guarantee, and the preservation of a functioning quorum in Congress, are the only aspects of Federal election management that have historically been in the Federal government's domain concerning elections, and the only ones that should continue to be matters of Federal oversight.

With the exception of correcting actual civil rights abuses and due process violations in elections, Congress has largely left states to decide their own voting processes since the enactment of the Constitution. For example, the 19th Amendment giving women the right to vote was not added to the U.S. Constitution until 1920; but Wyoming allowed women to vote beginning in 1890. Several other states followed Wyoming's lead before 1920 because these states exercised their own discretion in the 'manner of holding elections' by permitting women to vote. Georgia retains the discretion to require candidates to obtain 50 percent of the vote, plus one, or submit to a runoff election; most other states do not use this runoff method.

In 2021, some Members of Congress sought to enlarge the meaning of Article One, Section 4 well beyond the maintenance of due process and equality of access. A Federal law was proposed mandating little or no voter identification requirements, mandating unregulated voter drop-off boxes, ballot harvesting, possibly allowing extension of suffrage to non-citizens, and prohibitions on state efforts to update and correct voter registration rolls. This legislation failed narrowly, but constitutional confusion over election management should be eliminated in a manner retaining state preeminence in elections, unless they are found to have abused this plenary allocation of power. Thus:

AN AMENDMENT BY REVISION OF ARTICLE ONE, SECTION 4, PARAGRAPH #1:

"The Times, Places and Manner of holding Elections for Senators and Representatives, shall be **managed and** prescribed in each State by the Legislatures **and Courts** thereof; but the Congress may at any time by Law make or alter such Regulations *to ensure the presence of Congressional quorums, and to enforce provisions of this Constitution.* ~~except as to the Places of choosing Senators.~~ *The states may adopt different manners and processes for conducting elections, but no state shall enact election laws depriving eligible citizens of the United States of the right to vote or depriving them of due process under the law. The right to vote shall be restricted to citizens of the United States, as citizenship shall be defined by Congress. State and Federal courts may overturn individual elections and call for new or special elections where due process is found to have been abridged on a scale sufficient to warrant new elections."*

[17] Mitigate radical political partisanship by reducing Gerrymandering and thereby increase the number of competitive Congressional races.

Gerrymandering has become so advanced and is used so cynically by both political parties to protect incumbents and retain electoral majorities, that less than a fifth of Congressional races are actually competitive. For its part, the Supreme Court has been reluctant to weigh-in and correct this aberration in all but the most egregious Gerrymandering cases because they believe re-districting is an inherently political decision reserved to state legislatures. Blue states Gerrymander to give Democrats lopsided advantages, and Red states Gerrymander to give Republicans lopsided advantages. With so few competitive Congressional races in general elections, candidates have more to fear from electoral challenges in their respective party primaries.

This situation is undemocratic and shifts power to political party elites. It makes elections more radically Left or Right, thereby exacerbating political polarization and partisanship.

While some states have enacted non-partisan or bipartisan commissions to redraw Congressional districts, the steam has recently gone out of these efforts because each party perceives that advancing such solutions will put their party at a disadvantage during the next election cycle. Too many Congressional district maps look like a salamander or an octopus and artificially divide populations in a common region, trade area, or cultural group in the interests of obtaining partisan election outcomes. Those in power are disinclined to fix the problem because they are beneficiaries of the Gerrymandered dysfunction. For this reason, a constitutional amendment is likely the only way to comprehensively achieve redistricting reform.

AN AMENDMENT BY ADDING A NEW SECTION 5 TO ARTICLE FOUR:

"After each decennial census conducted in accordance with Article One, Section 2 of this Constitution, every state shall appoint a commission of citizens to draw-up new congressional and state legislative district boundaries. Each commission shall have equal representation from each of the political parties comprising at least 15% of the vote in the most recent gubernatorial election held in the state. Each commission shall create contiguous districts with comparable numbers of citizens in a manner that, to the greatest extent possible, retains in whole the various distinct regions of the state within the same district, minimizes the use of narrow connecting corridors, combines geographically adjacent

populations, and possesses contiguity and geographic compactness. The legislatures of each state shall only be authorized to accept or reject the recommendations of the commission without amendment."

[18] Replace or amend the Electoral College.

The first constitutional convention's "Great Compromise" reconciled large state and small state interests; it made the eventual adoption of the new Constitution possible through the creation of what is essentially a power-sharing agreement between sparsely populated states and states with greater numbers of residents. Without it, smaller states would have been at the mercy of larger states (then Virginia, Pennsylvania, and Massachusetts; now the three largest states are California, Texas, and Florida). The Electoral College is one of the pragmatic outcomes of the "Great Compromise;" another is equal representation for each state, regardless of population, in the U.S. Senate.

The United States doesn't really have national elections every four years to elect a president. They have fifty separate state elections which are aggregated to select the next president through the mechanism of the Electoral College. This infrequently makes it possible for the winner of the Electoral College vote to not be the winner of the popular vote. It also means the Federal government cannot usurp the process of selecting the president. The Founders intended that States remain paramount in selecting the president and vice-president. The "Great Compromise" gave smaller states slightly more "say" in the election process because if members of the Senate and House of Representatives are combined, states with smaller populations secure greater per capita representation than states with larger populations. For example, based on 2020 census figures, California is America's largest state by population and has 52 Representatives and 2 U.S. Senators, for a total of 54

Members of Congress (giving them 54 Electoral College votes). California, therefore, has one Member of Congress for every 732,910 residents. But Wyoming (America's smallest state by population), with just 1 Representative and 2 U.S. Senators, for a total of 3 Members of Congress (and 3 Electoral College votes), has one Member of Congress for every 192,283 residents. Thus, while the principle of "one-man-one-vote" is foundational to democracy, it does not apply to the U.S. Senate or, therefore, to the Electoral College.

Whether the "Great Compromise" (balancing interests and power between large and small states) is still necessary for holding the Union together is a question for delegates to a Second Constitutional Convention to ponder. What has not changed, however, is that smaller states are still concerned about being pushed aside by large states. The "Great Compromise" (creating the Electoral College and providing for equal state suffrage in the Senate) was not a mistake; it reconciled rural and urban states, large states and small, so they could live together under one system of governance acceptable to all. The Founding Fathers never intended that the election of the president be made exclusively by popular vote. They instituted a system accounting for, and catering to, a collection of different state and regional interests.

The intention of "The Great Compromise" was to compel rural and urban interests to negotiate and compromise with each other—rather than just assemble sufficient votes to overwhelm the other. In the current polarized and partisan political environment, it is unlikely three-fourths of the states will ever vote to reduce each state's influence through adoption of a purely popular-vote presidential process. This barrier should not, however, keep the country from developing more democratic methods of selecting the president. Fixing, without abandoning, the Electoral College is complicated because it is intrinsically linked to the structure of a Senate comprised of two senators from each state, no matter how large or small the state.

The authors of the U.S. Constitution could never have envisioned the ballot counting disputes of the 21st Century; but the governance system they created in the 18th Century has, nonetheless, partially insulated modern America from election chaos—likely by accident. Imagine if the Florida ballot counting fiasco during the 2000 election had been extended to the entire country. Election irregularities and fraud have tainted elections since the start of the Republic, and for this reason, election officials should remain vigilant in improving election security laws. But at least the Electoral College isolates election irregularities to one or two states. Imagine the chaos if voting irregularity claims from the 2016 and 2020 elections were not limited to just a few states, but were national in scope. Thankfully the damage is usually limited to just a few states. This is the unanticipated "firewall benefit" provided by the Electoral College.

What might be in the realm of political possibility for amending the Electoral College system? If a purely popular vote system is off the table, what are the alternatives to moving closer to the country's "one-man-one-vote" principles without completely abandoning the idea of equal representation in the Senate and indirect election of the president and vice-president through the Electoral College? Below are four options.

Option One: Amend the Constitution to extend the Nebraska-Maine method to the entire country. This option already functions in Nebraska and Maine because Article One, Section 4 gave these states the discretion to institute the change. Laws enacted in Nebraska and Maine reject the "winner-take-all" method of awarding Electoral College votes and provide that their Electoral College votes be awarded based on voting in each Congressional district, AND by how the entire state votes. Each Congressional District awards one Electoral College vote, and the two Electoral College votes corresponding to the state's U.S. senators are awarded to the candidate winning the statewide popular vote. This alternative method mitigates the effect of "winner-take-all" allocations of Electoral College voting practiced by the other 48 states. Thus, if presidential candidate Smith wins the popular vote in Maine's First Congressional district but loses the popular vote in the state's Second Congressional District, and she loses the statewide vote, then she still gets one Electoral College vote, and the remaining three Electoral College votes are awarded to her opponent. Extending this rule to all 50 states requires this amendment:

AN AMENDMENT BY INSERTION INTO ARTICLE TWO, SECTION 1:

"Electoral votes shall be awarded by State and by Congressional district. The winner of each state shall receive electoral votes corresponding to the number of senators representing that state in the U.S. Senate; and the winner of each Congressional district shall receive one electoral vote."

Option Two: This option is similar to Option One, except that awarding of Electoral College votes would no longer include seats in the Senate—just seats in the House of Representatives, with one added for the District of Columbia. Instead of 538 Electoral College votes there would be 436, with 219 Electoral College votes required to elect the president. While more aligned with the popular vote, this option largely erases the impact of state parties and of statewide election efforts; it would likely be resisted for this reason. Election appeals to statewide interests in a national campaign would likely be dissipated in favor of giving more attention to large population centers, and this option would be the most vulnerable to adverse Gerrymandering effects. Regardless, this option also requires an amendment for adoption:

AN AMENDMENT BY INSERTION INTO ARTICLE TWO, SECTION 1:
"One Electoral College vote shall be awarded to the winner of each Congressional district, and the District of Columbia shall have one vote."

Option Three: Amend the constitution to dilute, but not eliminate, the "Great Compromise" regarding "equal suffrage in the senate." A foundational principle of the Constitution is that every state, no matter how small, is entitled to have representation in both houses of the national legislature. This tenet can be retained by slightly modifying each state's suffrage in the Senate—simultaneously making the Senate a little more representative, and doing the same to the Electoral College, while still preserving some advantage for smaller states. Different versions of this proposal have been floated for years. This amendment option makes the Senate slightly more representative by giving each state one, two, or three senators based on their respective populations.[27] Enacting this approach also requires new constitutional language completely replacing the first two paragraphs of Article One, Section 3:

---

[27] There are different ways of giving more representation to large states in the Senate. Larry Sabato (op. cit.) proposes only adding rather than adding **and** subtracting senators based on population. The concept is similar, and there are numerous variations.

AN AMENDMENT BY ADDITION TO ARTICLE ONE, SECTION 3:

"Every state shall have representation in the Senate. After each decennial census, the number of senators from each state shall be altered such that the top one-third of states by population shall each have three senators, the second or middle one-third of states by population shall each have two senators, and the lowest one-third of states by population shall each have one senator. The total number of Senators shall be equal to twice the number of states in the Union."

Option Four: Combine options one and three, or two and three, above. All of these options retain the Electoral College system and give slightly more voice to smaller states. They also retain election irregularity "firewalls" by continuing to conduct 50 separate elections. Both options reduce the possibility of a candidate winning without securing a popular vote victory among registered voters (but they do not eliminate this possibility).

[19] Re-write Article Five to delete the Constitution's prohibition of amendments altering "equal suffrage in the Senate," and make it easier to call future constitutional conventions.

As calls for an Article Five convention of states have increased, alternative proposals have been advanced to first amend Article Five itself to insert parameters regulating how such a convention should proceed. No such amendment is proposed here. Unwarranted fears that a convention of states will go off the rails will be mitigated after a Second Constitutional Convention is called, convenes, and establishes a body of precedent for future conventions. A modern convention of states will serve as a template for subsequent efforts to amend the Constitution via conventions—perhaps to such an extent that further amendments to Article Five regarding the calling of conventions are unnecessary. If, after a Second Constitutional Convention finishes its work, questions remain about how to convene and manage a convention of states, then Article Five amendments could be considered in the future. But Article Five requires timely amendment for completely different reasons.

The last two clauses of Article Five should be deleted because one deals with slavery and is antiquated, and the other clause is a barrier to reform of the Electoral College linked to changing "equal suffrage in the Senate." In short, if the Electoral College is to be retained AND amended in ways altering equal suffrage in the Senate, then revisions of Article Five are required before, or concurrent with, Electoral College revisions.

The current language of Article Five bars any attempt to address the issue of slavery by constitutional amendment until after 1808. Congress passed a law outlawing the African slave trade from and after January 1, 1808—although the trade continued illegally in parts of the South until the Civil War. The 1808 law did not prohibit domestic slave sales, and children born into slavery remained slaves until ratification of the 13th Amendment. This last clause of Article Five was also written to codify "equal suffrage in the Senate" as permanently as possible. An amendment deleting the final clauses of Article Five would be simple to draft but deleting 'equal suffrage in the Senate' language must either be predicated on the assumption a new amendment will be rapidly sent to States establishing an alternative method for electing the Senate, or revision of Article Five must occur simultaneously (as a companion amendment) with adoption of a new method of electing senators.

A Second Constitutional Convention should also revise Article Five so that calling another constitutional convention in the future is less difficult. The calling of a convention of states should not require threats of armed rebellion, the disintegration of political norms, or the collapse of civil order for 34 states to realize that constitutional amendments may be required to right the Ship of State. For this reason, Article Five could also be amended to allow for periodic conventions, at least once a century unless called by two-thirds of states in the meantime—even if delegates elect to make no changes at centenary conventions. All of the proposed Article Five fixes discussed above are consolidated into new language below:

AN AMENDMENT BY DELETION AND ADDITION OF LANGUAGE IN ARTICLE FIVE:

"The Congress, whenever two thirds of both Houses shall deem it necessary, shall propose Amendments to this Constitution, or, on the Application of the Legislatures of two thirds of the several States, shall call a Convention for proposing Amendments, which, in either Case, shall be valid to all Intents and Purposes, as Part of this Constitution, when ratified by the Legislatures of three fourths of the several States, or by Conventions in three fourths thereof, as the one or the other Mode of Ratification may be proposed by the Congress. "~~Provided that no Amendment which may be made prior to the Year One thousand eight hundred and eight shall in any Manner affect the first and fourth Clauses in the Ninth Section of the first Article; and that no State, without its Consent, shall be deprived of its equal Suffrage in the Senate.~~" *At minimum, Congress shall convene a convention of states for purposes of proposing amendments to this Constitution no less than once every 100 years commencing from the date of ratification of this Article Five amendment or the most recent convention."*

An antiquated provision located at the beginning of Article One, Section 9 of the Constitution also barring Congress from interfering in the slave trade prior to 1808 should likewise be deleted, and the elimination of this language could be consolidated with the above Article Five amendments in the same proposal.

[20] More than double the size of the House of Representatives, fixing the number of its members near 900; and giving the District of Columbia voting representation in the House, even though DC would still not be a state.

The country has become so large that few Americans have any connection with their Congressional representatives. Smaller districts, and more representatives, would make it easier for persons of limited means to run for Congress, and it would make it harder for special interest lobbyists to swing votes to their causes without broader public support. More members in the House of Representatives would also reduce the possibility that presidential candidates could win the Electoral College vote without also winning the popular vote, even if "equal suffrage in the Senate" is retained. There are 650 members in the British House of Commons—one for every 104,000 United Kingdom residents. Increasing the size of the House of Representatives to 900 members would still settle about 360,000 people into each

Congressional district. Such an increase in House membership would help bring "the Peoples' House" closer to The People.

The number of members in the House of Representatives is not stipulated in the Constitution; it was codified at 435 by an Act of Congress. Article One, Section 2 of the Constitution (dealing with the composition of the House of Representatives) contains much antiquated language. A revision of this section, increasing the size of the House of Representatives, removing antiquated language, and allowing rapid refilling of unscheduled vacancies by a state's Governor, might look something like this:

AN AMENDMENT BY REVISION OF ALL OF ARTICLE ONE, SECTION 2:

The House of Representatives shall be composed of *nine hundred and one* Members chosen every second Year by the People of the several States *by popular elections in the manner of each state.* ~~and the Electors in each State shall have the Qualifications requisite for Electors of the most numerous Branch of the State Legislature.~~ No Person shall be a Representative who shall not have attained to the Age of twenty-five Years and been seven years a Citizen of the United States, and who shall not, when elected, be an Inhabitant of that State in which he shall be chosen. Representatives and direct Taxes shall be apportioned among the several States which may be included within this Union, according to their respective numbers *such that each district has a comparable number of residents as all other districts in the same State, based on decennial enumerations of the population.* ~~which shall be determined by adding to the whole Number of free Persons, including those bound to Service for a Term of Years, and excluding Indians not taxed, three fifths of all other Persons.~~ The actual Enumeration shall be made within three Years after the first Meeting of the Congress of the United States, and within every subsequent Term of ten Years, in such Manner as they shall by Law direct. ~~The Number of Representatives shall not exceed one for every thirty Thousand, but~~ Each State shall have at Least one Representative. ~~and until such enumeration shall be made, the State of New Hampshire shall be entitled to choose three, Massachusetts eight, Rhode Island and Providence Plantations one, Connecticut five, New York six, New Jersey four, Pennsylvania eight, Delaware one, Maryland six, Virginia ten, North Carolina five, South Carolina five, and Georgia three.~~ When vacancies happen in the Representation from any State, the Executive Authority thereof shall *appoint a replacement Representative* ~~issue Writs of Election~~ to fill such Vacancies *until the next regular election.* The House of Representatives shall choose their Speaker and other Officers *from among its current membership*; and shall have the sole Power of Impeachment."

[21] Make elections more inclusive by making it easier for third parties and independents to participate in elections.

The Founding Fathers did not anticipate the growth and power of political parties—though they should have done so, since political parties formed before the ink was dry on the Constitution's parchment. In the aftermath of the Revolution, the Framers believed partisan differences would yield to patriotic attention to the common good. They were wrong. America's two-party system has contributed much to the polarization and political extremes present in the Modern Age.

Ranked choice voting and other measures (whose adoption has already occurred in some states and does not require the authorization of a constitutional amendment because election means and methods are within the purview of the states) will serve to mitigate radical extremes of the Left and Right; but radical factions polarizing the nation could be further softened if it was easier for independent (or third) parties, as well as independent and third party candidates, to obtain access to the ballot on the same basis as Democrats and Republicans.

At both the State and Federal level, Republican and Democrat parties have worked together to erect barriers to the formation of third parties and equal ballot access for independents and third parties. They have done this to preserve a strictly two-party system. It is unreasonable to expect Members of Congress, 99% of whom are Republicans or Democrats, to pass laws making it easier for third parties and independents to stand for election with equal standing to the two main parties; so a constitutional change is likely the only way to level the playing field, by adding a new Section 6 to Article Four (or this paragraph could be added to the new Article Four, Section 5 amendment creating independent commissions to draw legislative district boundaries [proposal #17 above], ending partisan Gerrymandering).

AN AMENDMENT BY INSERTION INTO ARTICLE FOUR:

"In the conduct of all elections, all parties and candidates shall be treated equally, and given equal access to ballots and elections. Each state shall create independent and bipartisan election commissions to supervise the administration of all elections held in each state."

<u>GROUP FIVE</u>: Amendments to basic rights concerning free speech, censorship, excessive punishments, access to firearms, and codifying ethical standards for elected and appointed government leaders

The Bill of Rights is foundational to American governance; it should be strengthened and retained with the fewest of modifications. Nevertheless, the following four revisions of the Bill of Rights seem the most pressing in the current political and imbalanced governance environment.

[22] Extend free speech requirements to 'Big Tech' and others in the private sector.

The tenets of free speech enshrined in the Constitution have historically been interpreted to constrain governments from limiting free speech rights of citizens who may possess alternative, even hostile, views to those of the government. But this First Amendment guarantee does not extend to the actions of private businesses. This was not a nationwide problem until the advent of Facebook, Twitter and other privately owned ubiquitous social media platforms that started out only as apolitical cyber forums where everyone could share their experiences and views. These platforms have recently become weapons of political propaganda, social indoctrination and censorship. The Constitution's First Amendment is so fundamental to the nation's ethos, that it is hazardous to venture into any revisions of this sacred language. But the constitutional "fix" for the current dilemma is simple, requiring only that the existing prohibition on the stifling of free speech by governments be extended to the private sector whenever private sector entities engage in providing information and communication services in the public square.

AN AMENDMENT OF THE FIRST AMENDMENT BY ADDITION OF LANGUAGE:
"nor shall publicly or privately owned and operated forums, engaged in the general dissemination of public information, information exchanges in non-proprietary settings, and gatherings accessible to and used by the general population, impose unequal or unreasonable limits on the exercise of free speech."

[23] Revise the Eighth Amendment to the Constitution to end the death penalty.

The death penalty is disproportionately applied to the poor and persons of color. The advent of modern forensic techniques has also demonstrated that a disturbing number of capital convictions were not committed by the person found guilty in court. Although the death penalty for a capital crime, after a fair trial, was not historically considered "cruel and unusual punishment," many states have since abolished the death penalty precisely because they decided that in this Modern Age it is both cruel and unusual—in part because it provides no recourse in the event new evidence is discovered reversing the decision of a trial court. The death penalty is also expensive. It is cheaper for a State to incarcerate a murderer for the rest of his life than it is to go through the endless legal appeals required to get to an execution. This change can be enacted with a small change to the existing language of the Eighth Amendment, as recommended by the late Justice John Paul Stevens:

AN AMENDMENT THROUGH INSERTION OF LANGUAGE INTO THE EIGHTH AMENDMENT:

"Excessive bail shall not be required, nor excessive fines imposed, nor cruel and unusual punishments *such as the death penalty* inflicted."

[24] Revise the Second Amendment to preserve the original intentions of this foundational right; but do so in a manner reflecting advances in modern weaponry, and agree that access to guns need not extend to certain minors, felons, and the mentally unstable.

The Second Amendment does not specifically say everyone has a right to own a gun. It says: "A well-regulated Militia, being necessary to the security of a Free State, the right of the people to keep and bear Arms, shall not be infringed." Opponents of the Second Amendment argue that gun proliferation and easy access to firearms has drastically increased violent gun-related deaths, and that firearms are substantially more lethal today than they were in the 18th Century. Proponents of the Second Amendment argue that rapidly rising crime require access to firearms so that law abiding citizens can protect themselves and their families, and because the Second Amendment serves as a bulwark against tyrannical governments seeking to oppress citizens. Both views include elements of truth.

The original purpose of the Second Amendment was to allow citizens to protect themselves (from wild animals, domestic rebellion, and if necessary, from foreign invaders), and serve as a populist method for reining-in tyrannical government—via armed uprisings if necessary. But the Constitution's authors could not have intended that citizen militias be staffed with violent felons and persons lacking the mental capacity to make intelligent decisions regarding the rules of armed engagement and the proper use of lethal weapons.

Revisions to the Second Amendment must find a middle path between the extremes of the political Right and Left if they expect to achieve popular approval. This middle path can be found in reconsidering and redefining the role of militias and how people serve in their ranks. This discussion should also rethink the original intentions of the authors and ratifiers of the Second Amendment, and of other constitutional provisions dealing with law enforcement.

Who can serve in state and local militias lying outside the reach of the Federal government? Who can possess weapons that advance the mission and goals of citizen militias? Can gun ownership be linked to militia eligibility? Is the nation willing to find a compromise policy regarding firearms that is both inclusive of civil rights concerns and addresses community safety? These are hard questions to answer when trust in the Federal government is so low; but rising levels of gun violence require some action anyway. Here is one solution:

INSERT AND DELETE LANGUAGE WITHIN THE TEXT OF THE SECOND AMENDMENT:

"A well-regulated Militia, being necessary to the security of a free State, the right of *State and local militias and their members* ~~the people~~ to keep and bear Arms, shall not be infringed. *State and local militias shall be subject to this Constitution, but the Congress shall make no laws infringing on State authority to regulate the keeping and bearing of Arms by militia members, or who shall be qualified to serve as militia members.*

This language attempts to accomplish what may be impossible in the current Age—finding common ground on gun policies and support for state and local law enforcement. The language above does not mean only military reservists could have guns. On the contrary, it could result in action by state governments to issue permits for firearms to anyone over the age of 21 who is not a felon, has passed a background check, engages in regular gun training and practice, and is willing to be available for emergency call-ups to augment local law enforcement in the event of community violence. At a time when crime is on the increase across the country, having a large group of law-abiding citizens in every community trained and willing to loan their firearms expertise to improve community safety would bring more stability to crime distressed localities. To make certain no state adopts discriminatory rules for gun permit issuance, relief could still be sought through the courts under existing anti-discrimination provisions of the Constitution.

Under this new rubric, the term "militia" would take on a broader definition—meaning anyone qualified to serve as part of an on-call local defense group—outside Federal control. Expanding what is covered by the word "militia" will likely re-open the subject of the authority of state and local law enforcement as provided in the Constitution. Some in Congress would like to nationalize the police, and the Constitution does not definitively address this issue. Article One, Section 8 of the Constitution gives Congress the power "to provide for organizing, arming, and disciplining the Militia, and for governing such part of them as may be employed in the Service of the United States, reserving to the States respectively, the Appointment of the Officers, and the Authority of training the Militia according to the discipline prescribed by Congress." Since this provision was implemented in 1789, the Federal government has created a national police department (the Federal Bureau of Investigation), and several other domestic law enforcement agencies with authority to operate nationwide, and dealing with drug enforcement, border security, aviation security, park security, etc.—all having powers of arrest and detention. Their authority vis-à-vis state and local police and militias has never been entirely clear, and state and local authority over law enforcement has gradually eroded.

If all the powers of domestic civilian law enforcement are eventually vested in the central government, it will be increasingly difficult for state and local partners in the governance process to stop the drift to an all-powerful unitary government in Washington, DC. Accordingly, another small, but directly related, constitutional change warrants consideration by a convention of states as it concerns armed militias and state-level law enforcement:

AN AMENDMENT INSERTING A NEW SENTENCE INTO THE EXISTING LANGUAGE OF ARTICLE FOUR, SECTION 4:

"Absent such an application, or other formal agreement with a state, Federal law enforcement agencies are not permitted to usurp state and local law enforcement agencies except as may be expressly and directly authorized by an Act of Congress, approved by the president, and then only if the state or local government is in armed rebellion, civil order therein has collapsed, or they are violating provisions of this Constitution."

[25] Restore trust in government by enacting constitutional provisions ensuring government service is not self-enriching for national elected and senior appointed officials.

It may or may not be a fundamental right, but citizens are certainly entitled to know that the people entrusted with governing are not themselves personally profiting from their public positions. Changes could include rules prohibiting Members of Congress from receiving compensation for lobbying and other government influencing jobs for an extended period after their public service terms have ended, along with an Article One, Section 9 prohibition on the enactment of laws treating Members of Congress differently than all other citizens concerning employee benefits and other compensations (or through an addition to the 27th Amendment). It should also penalize the use of insider information for personal gain. For trust to be restored in the Federal government, citizens would likely favor language saying:

> *AN AMENDMENT THROUGH ADDITION OF A NEW 28*TH *AMENDMENT, OR BY ADDING THE SAME LANGUAGE TO THE 27*TH *AMENDMENT, AS FOLLOWS:*
> *"Members of Congress shall not use information obtained from their public position to make personal investment decisions; they shall not pass laws concerning their own compensation and benefits which are different from those available generally to all other citizens; and they shall be barred from employment for which they draw a salary or other form of compensation for lobbying any branch of the*

Federal government for a period of at least ten years following their last term of government service."

Amendments That Should Never Be Amendments

The twenty-five proposed amendments above are enough to begin robust discussions about ways to modernize and improve the Constitution. But this chapter does not include all constitutional topics raised in contemporary writings and media op-eds because some ideas for revising the Constitution simply should not appear on the agenda of a convention of states.

The subjects below are '**Amendments that should never be Amendments**.' They should never become constitutional amendments because the policy objectives of each can be achieved with an Act of Congress instead of a constitutional amendment, or the amendment idea is unwarranted, or the topic is satisfactorily addressed by other amendment proposals.

[A] End the disproportionate impact of "Dark Money" in elections.

"Dark Money" describes anonymous campaign contributions made in such volumes they tip the scales in elections, granting undue electoral influence on wealthy donors. Calls for constitutional reform on this topic stem from the 2010 *Citizens United v. Federal Election Commission* (FEC) decision striking down FEC rules as unwarranted limitations on free speech. This case was about the plaintiff's desire for unrestricted free speech, and the defendant's desire to keep wealthy campaign donors from corrupting the election process. But if a film critical of Hillary Clinton can be barred from the airwaves because it is too close to the election, then regulations on other types of political advertising could be next. The political party in control of the FEC could enact rules restricting the speech of opposing political groups. On the other hand, last-minute gossip about a candidate can be allowed to flood the Internet and airwaves if it is sufficiently bankrolled, even if it is slanderous and libelous. On the other hand, if a new advertisement is salacious AND true, doesn't the public have a right to know?

The courts have long ruled that freedom of speech is so sacred, so fundamental to a functioning democracy, that retaining free speech is worth the risk of allowing some untruths to circulate. But the solution to "dark money" problems does not require a constitutional amendment in the first place. Congress has the power to enact laws requiring greater transparency and disclosure of election funding sources. Furthermore, if constitutional proposal #16 (above) concerning the conduct of Federal elections is ratified, and dark money and/or other election corruption is found to have occurred to such an extent that it poisoned or altered an election outcome, a court of competent jurisdiction could provide a remedy by ordering a new or special election.

[B] End the use of empty shell bills in Congress.

Empty shell bills, filled-in after their approval and after few legislators have actually read and critiqued them, are the tools of tyrants. It has now become commonplace for Acts of Congress to be approved before they are fully written—leaving the details of law-making to legislative aids and unelected bureaucrats. This is an unethical abdication of Congressional responsibility. But correcting this practice only requires an Act of Congress to fix.

An amendment to the Constitution should only be offered (or a Third Constitutional Convention called) if Congress fails to self-correct this aberration.

[C] Codify a right to privacy.

The 2022 *Dobbs v. Jackson* decision determined there is no explicit and constitutional 'right to privacy' protecting a right to abortion in the Constitution. However, the 4th, 9th and 14th Amendments contain language suggesting that in many aspects of life unrelated to actual governance and civic duty, people are essentially entitled to be left alone. The *Dobbs v. Jackson* case reasserted the right of democratically elected legislatures (and not courts) to determine when there was a compelling public interest to protect the lives of unborn children from life-ending abortion procedures. *Dobbs* did not terminate other privacy rights. Nonetheless, this controversial decision has re-ignited discussions about whether there needs to be a constitutional amendment protecting privacy.

Privacy protections for doctor and attorney client privileges, maintenance of medical records privacy, other personal health decisions, and proprietary business information could be the subject of a constitutional amendment protecting personal privacy, but it is not necessary because the same protections can be achieved by Acts of Congress, and many of these privacy categories are already protected by law and have not been ended by the *Dobbs* decision.

Amendments to the Constitution should not be pursued if an Act of Congress will achieve the desired goal; the latter is easier to change and enact. Amendments to the Constitution should be reserved for actions necessary to balance the three branches of government, permanently secure rights and liberties to the people, correct antiquated provisions of the original Constitution, and enact key provisions that have, over time, shown they are resisted and opposed by Congress but are supported by the people (as demonstrated by the actions of three-fourths of their legislatures).

[D] Bring back the Equal Rights Amendment in a Different Form.

Few people disagree with the original reasons for an Equal Rights Amendment; but the concern over its 'unintended consequences' remains. The reason this amendment has no future is that many of the ERA's women empowerment objectives have been achieved without passage of the amendment, and because in the 2020s, references to sex and gender by those considering constitutional revisions will unavoidably be extended to alternative sexual identities—thus becoming a catalyst to use the Constitution for enlarging the rights of creative, innovative, and unscientific gender categories. For this reason, a new-ERA would have no chance of achieving support from 38 states. Drop this proposal from any convention agenda because recriminations and posturing over gender issues could poison other work products emerging from a Second Constitutional Convention.

[E] Immigration Policy.

The failure of the Federal government to adopt rational immigration policies is simply a failure of governance. The political Right believes the country's immigration policy can be limited to building walls and keeping almost everyone out—even in the midst of an unprecedented national labor shortage. The political Left advocates for unsecure, open, and porous borders, creating chaos, increasing crime and the flow of drugs, and making a mockery of the rule-of-law. The two sides should stop posturing and using this issue for political fund raising; they should find a compromise best suited to the country. With few exceptions, the Legislative and Executive Branches of the Federal government already possesses the authority to legislate in this area under terms already contained in the Constitution. Congress should exercise this authority and fix the nation's broken immigration system without further delay; no constitutional revisions are needed to enact comprehensive and bipartisan immigration reform.

Postscript

Not long ago, while waiting in line at a shop in Decatur, Illinois, I overheard a customer tell his companion, "If the government really cared about people, everyone would know how to swim." This statement may mirror the views of millions of Americans; if not about swimming, or operating a car, or the politically correct view of sex education, then some other parochial indicator. Millions of citizens probably believe it is the government's job to teach everyone to swim, raise their children, or direct and manage other critical parts of life. Sadly, a sizeable percentage of citizens may have even formed an opinion of their government based on such flimsy metrics. By contrast, millions of other Americans do not agree; they believe teaching critical life-lessons is the responsibility of parents and individuals outside government. This yawning government expectations gap continues to widen; the growing chasm contributes to the political divide now tearing at the fabric of American culture. There is a vast difference in what Americans believe should be the purpose, roles, and functions of their government.

The responsibilities of government are listed in the Constitution's Preamble: "establish justice, ensure domestic tranquility, provide for the common defense, promote the general welfare, and secure the blessings of liberty to ourselves and our posterity." State and Federal governments have added much to this list since 1787. In the 21ˢᵗ Century, the Federal government has come to dictate societal norms in troublesome ways, usurp state discretion, and threaten individual freedoms and liberty. Governance in the 21ˢᵗ Century should not look like 18ᵗʰ Century governance; and State and Federal governments should do more for citizens than they did in 1787. But they should do so in ways retaining and maintaining "balance of power" and "limited government" principles.

The authors of the Constitution were mostly Protestants, well-read in the Christian philosophy of their time. It taught that worldly governments exist principally to provide order on this side of Heavenly Glory, while awaiting the Second Coming of Christ.[28] In short, since all humans are sinners, the task of earthly governments is limited mainly to establishing order and preventing people from killing each other until the advent of a spiritual kingdom where Christ rules. The Founding Fathers were also schooled in the works of major Enlightenment thinkers (Montesquieu, Rousseau, Voltaire) who argued for separated government powers and for barriers to the exercise of tyranny and arbitrary actions by courts, legislatures, and executives. In the 18ᵗʰ Century, these ideas were mostly compatible with the Protestant worldview, and with the widely influential *Declaration of the Rights of Man and of the Citizen*, published in France in 1789. These principles emerge from the first paragraph of the Declaration of Independence, where Jefferson asserts concepts so fundamental to human existence that they should be considered universally applicable.

This overarching commitment to limited government and containment of natural avarice derive from Enlightenment

---

[28]   Isaiah 9:6-7; John 18:36; Romans 13:1-7; I Corinthians 15:24-27; I Peter 2:13-17.

philosophies; but they are no longer prevalent in 21ˢᵗ Century society. Limited government is no longer a default position 21ˢᵗ Century citizens assume, accept, or fully understand. The Preamble of the Constitution remains in place, but its philosophical foundations have been eroded. If the nation wishes to re-assert a modern operational definition of limited government, it cannot expect to rely on 18ᵗʰ Century political doctrines buttressed by Protestant theology. Re-asserting a philosophy of limited government (if in fact that is what the country desires) requires codification in the form of thoughtfully constructed new provisions of constitutional text.

To restore balance, either American government needs to be reset by restoring the safeguards that sustained limited government until the middle of the 20ᵗʰ Century, or new philosophies of governance should replace the ones that have supported American Exceptionalism since 1789. Either way, an Article Five convention is the only legal and peaceful mechanism for making the revisions. The Framers wrote Article Five for precisely the turning point of political circumstances and governance dysfunction the United States now faces.

Is this really necessary?

Yes, because the Federal government should live within its means.

Yes, because the Federal government should not be permitted to practice extortion and blackmail by refusing to remit funds raised through taxation from states until the same states agree to abide by regulations that have not been adopted by Congress and are beyond the Federal government's enumerated powers.

Yes, because only democratically elected legislatures should be empowered to make laws and raise taxes.

Yes, because American governance can still be made more accessible and more democratic.

Yes, because America is worth saving.

Why does it matter?

If the American people are denied an opportunity to adapt and revise their Constitution only because it is too hard to get amendments approved (it has been more than 50 years since three-fourths of the states voted to ratify a new amendment); and if Congress lacks the political will to make broadly supported policies and to legislate for the nation—kicking more legislative decisions to the courts and making nine unelected persons both too powerful and too politicized to effectively resolve key disputes and safeguard the Constitution, then the political system starts breaking down. Some would argue that it is already breaking down.

I appeal to you, reader, to use this book to advocate for a new convention of states. The need for, and the promise of, a Second Constitutional Convention is a topic that should be raised in future state legislative contests—particularly in states that have not already adopted contemporary resolutions calling for an Article Five convention.

Appendix "A"

Status of Constitutional Convention Applications

States that have contemporaneously passed a Convention of States application (19, as of this book's publication):

1. Georgia March 6, 2014

2. Alaska April 19, 2014

3. Florida April 21, 2014

4. Alabama May 22, 2015

5. Tennessee February 4, 2016

6. Indiana February 29, 2016

7. Oklahoma April 25, 2016

8. Louisiana May 25, 2016

9. Arizona March 13, 2017

10. North Dakota March 24, 2017

11. Texas May 4, 2017

12. Missouri May 12, 2017

13. Arkansas February 14, 2019

14. Utah March 5, 2019

15. Mississippi March 27, 2019

16. Wisconsin January 25, 2022

17. Nebraska January 28, 2022

18. West Virginia March 4, 2022

19. South Carolina March 29, 2022

Appendix "B"

Nebraska Resolution Applying
for a Convention of States

Nebraska 107th Legislature Second Session

LEGISLATIVE   **RESOLUTION**   **14**
FINAL READING

Introduced by Halloran, 33; Bostelman, 23; Brewer, 43; Briese, 41; Clements, 2; Erdman, 47; Friesen, 34; Gragert, 40; Hansen, B., 16; Kolterman, 24; Lindstrom, 18; Linehan, 39; Lowe, 37; McDonnell, 5; Murman, 38; Slama, 1; Williams, 36; Hilkemann, 4; Flood, 19.

Read first time January 08, 2021 -- Committee: Government, Military and Veterans Affairs

NOW, THEREFORE, BE IT RESOLVED BY THE MEMBERS OF THE ONE HUNDRED SEVENTH LEGISLATURE OF NEBRASKA, SECOND SESSION:

1. The Legislature of the State of Nebraska hereby applies to Congress, under the provisions of Article V of the Constitution of the United States, for the calling of a convention of the states limited to proposing amendments to the Constitution of the United States that impose fiscal

restraints on the federal government, limit the power and jurisdiction of the federal government, and limit the terms of office for its officials and for members of Congress.

2. The Clerk of the Legislature shall transmit copies of this application to the President and Secretary of the United States Senate, to the Speaker and Clerk of the United States House of Representatives, to the members of the Senate and House of Representatives from this state, and to the presiding officers of each of the legislative houses in the several states, requesting their cooperation.

3. This application constitutes a continuing application in accordance with Article V of the Constitution of the United States until the legislatures of at least two-thirds of the several states have made applications on the same subject.

4. This application will be rescinded as of February 1, 2027.

*Legislative advocacy by the Convention of States Project (conventionofstates.com) has resulted in adoption of joint resolutions by 19 states since 2014. Fifteen more are needed. The adopted Nebraska resolution is based on the Convention of States Project model. This model and the Nebraska resolution list the same three proposed amendment topics. The Convention of States Project model resolution reflects a politically conservative agenda, but Blue States can propose topics with liberal/progressive leanings too; because if 34+ states enact resolutions calling a convention of states, the resolutions and topics for amendment need not be identical. Debates in state legislatures about whether to call a convention of states have also mentioned changing the Electoral College, mitigating the impact of Gerrymandering and advancing other constitutional revisions generally more aligned with the political objectives of the Left. The Convention of States Project model calls for the making of "amendments" because the use of this language tracks with Article Five and because nearly identical language should make it harder for Congress to ignore 34+ calls for a second constitutional convention. Nonetheless, there is no requirement that individual State calls for a convention of states be identical or propose the same list of amendment topics.

About the Author

Scot Wrighton is a professional government manager and governance consultant. In addition to serving various local governments as a manager for three decades, he has served on the faculty of the University of Georgia's Carl Vinson Institute of Government, and he has worked internationally and domestically to advance good governance principles and techniques—as a consultant, instructor and project manager.

www.ingramcontent.com/pod-product-compliance
Lightning Source LLC
Chambersburg PA
CBHW070629030426
42337CB00020B/3958